The Blessings of Motherprayer

The BLESSINGS *of*

Motherprayer

SACRED WHISPERS
of MOTHERING

BARBARA MAHANY

Abingdon Press
Nashville

THE BLESSINGS OF MOTHERPRAYER
SACRED WHISPERS OF MOTHERING

Copyright © 2018 by Barbara Mahany

All rights reserved.

Library of Congress Cataloging-in-Publication Data has been requested.

ISBN 978-1-5018-5782-9

"Perhaps the World Ends Here", from THE WOMAN WHO FELL FROM THE SKY by Joy Harjo. Copyright © 1994 by Joy Harjo. Used by permission of W. W. Norton & Company, Inc. Additional permission to use the material has been granted by the author c/o The Permissions Company, Inc., www.permissions company.com.

Prayers of a Young Poet: Rainer Maria Rilke Translated and introduced by Mark S. Burrows, Copyright © 2013 by Mark S. Burrows. Used by permission of Paraclete Press. www.paracletepress.com

Material from *Slowing Time* (Copyright 2014 by Barbara Mahany) and *Motherprayer* (Copyright 2017 by Barbara Mahany) was used in *Blessings of Motherprayer*. Used by Permission. All rights reserved.

"A Litany of Remembrance" by Rabbi Sylvan Kamens and Rabbi Jack Reimer from *Gates of Repentance: The New Union Prayerbook for the Days of Awe*, copyright © 1978, revised 1996 by Central Conference of American Rabbis and Women of Reform Judaism, and are under the copyright protection of the Central Conference of American Rabbis and reprinted for use by permission of the CCAR. All rights reserved.

18 19 20 21 22 23 24 25 26—10 9 8 7 6 5 4 3 2 1
MANUFACTURED IN THE UNITED STATES OF AMERICA

This one is for my papa, who birthed in me the pure joy of words, who sat by my side in my darkest hours, and who dwells forever in my wellspring. And who never knew the loves of my life: Blair, Will, and Teddy.

Always, for every blessed soul who opens these pages. May sacred whisper find you.

Perhaps the World Ends Here

The world begins at a kitchen table. No matter what, we must eat to live.

The gifts of earth are brought and prepared, set on the table. So it has been since creation, and it will go on.

We chase chickens or dogs away from it. Babies teethe at the corners. They scrape their knees under it.

It is here that children are given instructions on what it means to be human. We make men at it, and we make women.

At this table we gossip, recall enemies and the ghosts of lovers.

Our dreams drink coffee with us as they put their arms around our children. They laugh with us at our poor falling-down selves and as we put ourselves back together once again at the table.

This table has been a house in the rain, an umbrella in the sun.

Wars have begun and ended at this table. It is a place to hide in the shadow of terror. A place to celebrate the terrible victory.

We have given birth on this table, and have prepared our parents for burial here.

At this table we sing with joy, with sorrow. We pray of suffering and remorse. We give thanks.

Perhaps the world will end at the kitchen table, while we are laughing and crying, eating of the last sweet bite.

—*Joy Harjo*

Contents

CONTENTS

Autumn: Season of Awe

A Note from My Kitchen Table

The weaving of this book, these pages, has been an exercise in joy, and the rediscovery of wonder and wisdoms and unanswerable questions, ones that held—and hold—my deepest attentions. Here and often, I draw from two wells deep inside, both of which seem never to run dry: the call of my soul to slow time, pay attention, savor what's holy, bow and bend knee in unfiltered gratitude; and, just as certainly, the unending explorations of mothering, that sacred oft-overlooked landscape that presses one heart hard up against another, the one that teaches essential lessons in loving—and living.

Love as you would be loved. Live as if tomorrow's not promised (because it isn't).

I entwine both here—slowing time, motherprayer—because one informs the other. One fuels the other's flame. And circles back again.

To mother with fullest heart, we need sustenance of the soulful sort. And how better to practice the sacred instruction—love without measure, without end, as inscribed in every ancient and timeless text—than to put it to work in the realm where mother and child together learn to find their way, twisting and turning through unmapped terrain, rising to heights not before imagined and lows that dredge the bottomless canyon?

It's messy, all right, and bumpy, too, but it's the surest equation I know in which one life launches another, and courage and love and endless prayerful implorings are essential for flight. Heavenly flight.

First, though, our eyes, our ears, our hearts, and our souls must be opened. Only then can the light—the wisdom and wonder—find its way in, in through the pried-open channels, even in through our brokenness. Maybe especially through our brokenness.

The hope stitched into each loop of word-thread in these pages is that the joy of discovery and rediscovery is "catching," as my grandmama used to say. That you'll catch a case of that joy, that you'll relish what you find here, that one smidge of a morsel—be it short, medium, long, or longer—might be just what you need to sustain you. To carry you through the dry patches of the day, the arid hours of the soul, to quench your heart's thirst, to quell your deepest yearnings.

Some years ago, before I began a writing practice-turned-spiritual practice of trying to capture the wonder and wisdoms of every blessed day, I wrote what amounted to a credo. It's as true today as it was back when I first tapped out these words:

We are looking for everyday grace. I believe that in quietly choosing a way of being, a way of consciously stitching Grace and Beauty into the whole cloth of our days, we can sew love where before there was only one moment passing into another. Making the moment count, that's what it's about here. Inhaling, and filling our lungs and our soul with possibility. Learning to breathe again. Learning to listen to the quiet, blessed tick and the tock of our heart. Steeping our soul in purest light so that, together, we can shoosh away the darkness that tries always to seep in through the cracks, wherever they might be. Please, pull up a chair.

A decade later, I circled back in that way that history and science beckon us: to take measure, to assess, to divine truths, to determine whether our hypothesis—our hope—has stood the test of time. I was not let down.

Everyday grace, surely, is the shimmering something we've found, the holiest thing. It's there when you look, when you pay close attention. But it's so easily missed. You need to attend to your post in the watchtower of life. Need to be on the lookout, ever on the lookout. You've no idea where or when it will come, the everyday grace. It doesn't arrive with trumpet blast, nor even a rat-a-tat drumroll. True grace is not seeking applause. Simply the certain knowledge that it's just brushed by, grazed against the contours of your heart and your soul. And it leaves you, every time, just a little bit wiser, a little more certain that Holy is all around.

The quiet we set out to find, it infuses every square inch. In a world torn at the seams by incivility, in a world where, day after day, tenderness is trampled under the hard boot heels of hate and bullying and a toughen-up attitude, we stay gentle. We trade, ardently, in tenderness. We hold up a radiant grace, a blessedness that stitches hearts into a whole.

Never more so than deep in the heart of motherlove—that inexhaustible yet exhausting devotion, unlike any other, the one sealed from the get-go, the one from which there is no escape. It's living-breathing prayer (motherprayer, motherlove, motherfaith) played out in words and beyond words—the verbs of loving attention: to feed, to cradle, to tend, and to attend, a mere sampling—as we love in ways never before beheld. Love our own, yes, *and* love those beyond the walls of the shelter we call home. For motherlove is grace, is balm, is so deeply needed in every nook and cranny of this sorry, shaken world.

Motherlove. It just might be God's most breathtaking invention.

What's offered here, in these pages, is distilled, extracted, as a syrup boiled down from the maple tree's vernal drippings, sweet essence that comes from long, slow simmering. The whole point is to dip in—a teaspoon, a ladle, or even a pot with a lid. Take what you please. Pause. Consider. Go on with your everyday hustle and bustle.

I've unfurled the snippets and threads as the calendar year unfolds, across the arc of the seasons, blessed beautiful seasons, pausing to consider certain holy days and holidays. I've woven in Wonderlists, and Count-Your-Blessings Calendars, a compendium of blessings that amount to meditative Post-its. I've slipped in a seasonal recipe or two, unearthed from the banged-up recipe tin that holds the relics of cooks and bakers and shortcut-takers I have loved. I've punctuated with prayer. (Often, for me, prayer is as much prose as it is poetry or straight-up petition, so what I call a prayer might be more like conversation, thinking aloud, or plain old talking, except I'm talking to God. And because I'm Christian—specifically, Catholic—and my husband is Jewish, our family encounters the Divine in the rituals and idioms of two faith traditions, and sometimes the prayers to which I turn are ones rooted in Hebrew text.) The prayers beyond words will be yours to live and breathe, as I live and breathe mine. And stitching this all together, making it whole, those swatches and threads of thought, notion, and words I might live by. Words that point me toward the holiness all around. And certainly the holiness that animates the blessed heart of mothering.

Because I've culled the pages of my first two books, *Slowing Time: Seeing the Sacred Outside Your Kitchen Door*, and *Motherprayer: Lessons in Loving,* and pulled out those lines and passages with particular resonance, the ones that draw me back for deeper pondering (in addition to weaving in whole new musings and thoughts and newborn prayers), this book might read a bit like you're peeking into my occasional jottings, something of a journal of the heart. I emphatically invite you in, and beg you to scribble in the margins, tuck in snippets and bits all your own. Make of this a living, breathing daily companion.

All in all, this is something of a patchwork. A patchwork of joy. Of love. Of wonderment. And it's the closest I've yet come to field notes on the blessings of motherprayer, fueled and put to flight on the wings of sacred whisper.

Newborn Year

Season of Beginnings Anew

*I*n the beginning, we start anew. As the shimmer of the festive days past begins to fade, as the newborn year begins its stirrings, we too breathe in fresh new air. Fill our lungs and our hopes and dreams, once again. Surrender to this chance to start all over again, a surrender born of humility, as we strip away old skin, tick through our litany of stumbles, our shortcomings. We make vows. Promise to try harder. Sketch dreams. Cast prayer upon the updraft. Especially our motherprayer, those vespers at the heart of who we are and how we love. We deepen in this season of long, dark nights, as minute by minute the light comes. Longer, fuller. Reaching from solstice toward equinox. The whole earth, and heavens too, echo our supplications. Our oath to love more fully, to live with the certitude that this time around, we'll inch closer to whom we were meant to be, whom we so deeply imagine. Whom God already sees.

Newborn Year's Wonderlist

it's the season of . . .

snow-laden sky creeping in unawares . . .

the red-cheeked badge of courage, come the close of a slow-spooled walk
through winter's woods . . .

frost ferns on the windowpanes . . .

snow falling first in feather-tufts, then fairy-dusted stars, and, finally,
prodigiously, in what could only be curds . . .

noses pressed to glass, keeping watch as winter's storm wallops . . .

soup kettle murmuring——slow, steady, hungrily . . .

pinecones crackling in the hearth . . .

mittens that dare to be lost, lest they're tethered to strings knotted and threaded
through coat sleeves . . .

scribble your own newborn wonders here . . .

A Count-Your-Blessings Calendar

Blessed Be the Newborn Year, Season of Beginnings Anew

NEW YEAR'S DAY (JAN. 1): Usher in the new year with a day of quietude; sunrise to sundown, hushed. Unplug. Slow simmer. Amble. May the loudest utterance be the turning of a page. Or the murmur of a tender kiss.

BLESSING 2: Weather lesson: In life, we are wise to keep ourselves stocked deep inside with whatever it takes to weather all that life throws our way. It is resilience with which we must line our inner shelves. And unswerving faith, stored in gallon jugs, to ride out any storm.

EPIPHANY (JAN. 6): Bundle up and take a moonwalk. Consider the gift of the nightlight that waxes and wanes but always guides our way. Pay attention to the moon's portion. Keep a moon journal, recording each night's lunar fraction, on the way toward wholeness or decline. What blessing, especially for a child. Isn't this the miracle of learning to marvel?

BLESSING 4: There is something mystical about the drama of a winter storm. You can't help but feel small as the sky turns marbled gray, the winds pick up, howl.

Trees commence their thrashing. It's a fine thing for the human species to remember the amplitude of what we're up against.

REV. DR. MARTIN LUTHER KING JR.'S BIRTHDAY (JAN. 15): Read the whole of Dr. King's "I Have a Dream" speech. Picture the world as you would dream it, then set out to make it real, one act of kindness at a time.

BLESSING 6: Take extra care to scatter cracked corn, peanut butter-smeared pine cones, and suet cakes for the loyal backyard critters who've settled in for winter, especially when arctic winds screech. Whisper thanks for those who keep watch on us.

BLESSING 7: Proffer consecration for the scarlet-cloaked cardinal——the one flash of pigment till Valentines flutter. He is the very heartbeat of promise, hope on a wing, a laugh-out-loud reminder that we are not alone. That red of reds shatters all that's bleak, shouts: "There is life where you are doubting."

CANDLEMAS (FEB. 2): Amid the winter's darkness, pause to consider the blessing of the candles, ordained to illuminate the hours. Fill your kitchen table, gathering a flock of orphan candlesticks. Adorn with winter branches and berries clinging to the bough.

BLESSING 9: Behold the hush of snowfall. The flakes free-falling past the porch light, their hard-angled intricacies and puffy contours tumbling, tumbling, lulling all the world and its weary citizens into that fugue state that comes with heavy snow——when at last we take in breath, and hold it. Fill our empty lungs.

BLESSING 10: Be dazzled by the diamond-dusted world you just woke up to. The way the flakes catch bits of

moonlight, shimmer like a thousand million stars. To be dazzled is a prayer.

VALENTINE'S DAY (FEB. 14):
Tuck love notes under pillows, inside
lunch bags and coat pockets. Sprinkle
a trail of construction-paper hearts from bedside to
breakfast table, and christen the day with whimsies and
joy. Murmur deep thanks for the gifts of heart.

BLESSING 12: Sometimes winter pushes us to the ends of
our hope. It can be the season of nearly giving up. But then
the holy hallelujah comes—the red bird, the pure contentment
of mere survival, the steaming bowl of soup when you come in
from shoveling, winter's Sisyphean folly.

BLESSING 13: Savor the sanctuary of being tucked in a cozy kitchen,
looking out at a winter world of which we stand in awe. Bless the contemplative
nature of this season that draws us into the depths of our cave, where we find fuel
for the seasons still to come.

BLESSING 14: Bundle up for a meandering walk in the end-of-winter woods,
marvel at the survival of so many species. Marvel at your own.

Letter to the New Year

Dear Year Soon-to-Crown,

As I've done before in birthing rooms, I will reach out to cradle you, take you in my hands, pull you close against my chest. You'll hear my heart beating, quietly.

I will study you, be in awe of your sudden appearance, your entrance, your being here. There was no guarantee you and I would meet, and therein is the miracle, the often-taken-for-granted miracle. Yet, unmistakably a miracle. In every way.

Both miracle and blessing, each new year demands my full and unwavering attention. Demands the full attention of all of us standing here on the cusp, filling our hearts and our imaginations with promises, vows, hopes, resolutions of the deepest kind.

I count on both hands and beyond the people I've loved—loved dearly—who didn't get to know you. The ones, especially, who missed you by a year, or two—the loss still raw, ever a mystery, one I'll never solve. They're the everyday reminder that this new year didn't have to be in my cards. Could have been eclipsed. Gone before I got here.

I can't shake the frame locked in my imagination, the one of my dear friend last March, lying gaunt in her hospital bed, all the tubes finally taken away. There was no need for tubes anymore; they'd been revealed to be false hope, distraction from the inevitable. She looked up at me, asked, thinly, "Can you believe this?" Her words as much declaration as question. I think of her on the doorstep of death, breaths away from slipping to the other side. I hold that moment. Study it. I breathe in her courage; I pray it infuses every last nook and cranny inside me. I pray I live her dying instruction: "Practice gratitude."

I beg you, new-coming year, to be gentle. Maybe you won't be. I realize the gentle needs to come from deep inside me. I need to find the holy balm to steady me through the rough waters to come. I'm bracing myself with double doses of those few things that have proven to be my salvation: prayer; silence; rampant and unheralded kindness; the rapt company of a rare few companions, deep in the act of holding up each other's hearts.

I will usher you in with all the majesty a new year deserves: I'm quieting already. I'm taking walks in the woods, standing in awe of the crimson flash of the flicker darting from oak to oak. I'm assuming a prayerful pose under the star-embroidered dome of the heavens. I awake with the dawn, press my nose to the window, often step outside, watch the tourmaline streaks stain the eastern edge of night, rise up, rinse the morning sky in diffuse and certain light.

I will curl in my armchair and scribble my own list of promises. The ways I hope to be kind. To be gentle. To forgive. To try and try again.

The dawn of each year draws me into my natural monastic state. I would have been such a cheerful monk, walking the moonlit halls, bare feet slapping the great stone slabs, guided by a flickering candle's flame. I would have relished a bowl of bean soup simmered all New Year's Eve Day. Would have sliced a thick baton of wheatberry bread. Alas, I'm without monastery walls at this moment in my life and thus must do without the stone-slabbed corridors. But I've beans and bread and bees' wax. I've a heart awaiting the new year, and all the prayers it will stir.

Be gentle, New Year. Be kind. And most of all, be blessed.

On Lessons from Mothering

I. Love as You Would Be Loved

From the start, the moments that enveloped me most, the ones out of which the deepest inklings were born, were the moments that felt bigger, much bigger, than me. These were the moments that pulsed with questions that ultimately ask, how do we love? How, truly, do we love? How do we press against the bounds of what we thought our hearts could do and discover, blessedly, the capacity for more?

To mother a child—by birth or by heart, by accident or happenstance or long-held dream—is to encounter love in ways never before beheld. In ways that stretch you, sometimes break you, build you up, and mightily and often demand the best that you can be.

Lessons learned in motherhood's ineluctable front lines serve as a paradigm for loving far beyond our lifeblood.

To learn to mother—to learn *from* mothering—is to learn to love in the ways of Jesus and Gandhi and Mother Teresa and Martin Luther King Jr., and even Louisa May Alcott's Marmee. It is to love as instructed in the Gospel, the Torah, the Qur'an, and every holy book ever inscribed: love as you would be loved.

Along the course of motherhood, I've studied hard the love lessons offered.

I was intent on teaching myself how to love—unconditionally and without waver—in ways I'd longed to love and be loved.

I did the one wise thing I know when nothing but abyss lay before me: I unreeled my prayer, set petitions to the wind, counting on those pleas to find the ears, the heart, the soul of Holy Tender God.

I prayed my way home, time after time.

And in the whisperings that stirred my soul and set me on my way, I did learn a thing or two. Learned what it means to love and love deeply. Learned how much it sometimes hurts. Learned just how brave I might be—if pushed, and if my kid's life (or heart or soul) depends on it.

II. Mothering Matters

Mothering matters. Life-and-death matters. Whole-or-empty matters.

Mothering matters in those hours when someone you love is at the end, the very end, of his or her rope. When that someone is near despondent with hopelessness. Or maybe just burning with fever.

Mothering matters, too, in all the in-between times. The barely noticed times. The I-remember-you-love-this-jelly-more-than-the-other-kind times. The you-missed-the-bus-again?! times; Oh-sure-I'll-drive-you times . . .

To mother, in the way that I mean, is to become the vessel that your child, your someone who loves you, needs. Not in a hollowed-out, I'm-nothing sort of a way. But in a mighty, I'll-be-what-you-need, I'll-be-*whatever*-you-need sort of a way. Or I'll try anyway.

It is to be living, breathing empathy.

Can you even begin to imagine the job description?

Try this: must be willing, for the duration, to cradle against the harshest winds, cruel winds, winds hell-bent on knocking over the someone you love. Must be alert to cries in the night. And ones at the end of long-distance phone lines. Must be able, without warning, to execute basic first-aid skills (kisses to cuts and bumps, bee stings, and bruised egos required). Must be willing to lie, wide-eyed and heavy-hearted, for long hours, sometimes from midnight till daybreak, pondering the conundrum of the day.

Not-quite-optional: be adept at celebrating small triumphs, ones that no one else might notice, but you know because you've been listening and watching, and you've seen how steep was the path your loved one was climbing. Must let go—not of the heart, but *eventually* of the hands-on role in everyday choices, the small stuff, sometimes even the big stuff. Must witness (wincing or not) the making of mistakes (and be willing to admit your own). Must try not to snap or to scold (*scolding*, a verb some of us might have grown up with, does nothing but chafe at the soul, nip at the bud of the blossoming, beautiful child). Must forgive. Yourself and your someone you love.

III. The Sacred Heart of Mothering

Maybe in thinking hard and deep and ponderously about the lessons that motherhood demands we struggle through, we might look down one day and see that our heart has grown deeper and wider and wiser than we ever imagined. Maybe we're one iota closer to the glorious magnificence we were meant to be.

Maybe we've learned from this one sacred heart—the heart of our child, from whom we can't, and won't, walk away—just how it might be to be fiercely and tenderly and infinitely loved, in that way that I believe we are loved by God almighty. And meant to love, most certainly.

Just maybe, in exploring motherhood, its interior and its borders, in illuminating the ledge where we let go and turn it over to the updraft I call prayer, maybe in imploring, begging, believing in the tender arms that will not let us—or our children—hurtle into the bottomless nothingness, we'll find God in depths and intimacies we've never known. Or imagined. God who loves us as a mother loves. God who hears the cries of our heart, from down the shadowed corridor, in deep of night. God who keeps the watch light burning, and will not abandon the vigil, not until we find our way through the darkness.

It's in knowing this God that we'll wrap ourselves more freely and more fervently in the shawl of prayer, motherprayer, those utterances that come from our most stripped-down essence. In knowing this God who is fluent in a mother's love, aren't we opening a channel that joins our heart to God's?

Motherhood, it seems, has caught me in its everlasting grip. No other instruction—sacred or otherwise—has so captivated, enchanted, or ignited me.

Nor so blessed me.

Blessings for Starting Anew

*D*eep in the truth of all of us lies the rough draft that demands edit after edit.

And so we are blessed, those of us who keep time, who trace the day, the week, the year in spiral. Who bow down to this new beginning.

It is, at heart, a geometry of promise, hope, and, most of all, ascension. It offers us the chance, over and over, to come back to that sacred moment when we stand at the crest of the hill, cast arms wide, salute the heavens, shake off dirt and dust, remap our route, and see if this time 'round we might inch higher toward the summit.

I don't know a world religion that doesn't devote a chapter, at least, to absolution, cleansing, rinsing. It is as if we are hardwired for holy resurrection. To rise from our brokenness. To seek forgiveness for our sins and shortcomings. To come back to the fresh start, the blank slate, to try and try again. To believe in the almighty "take two."

And so it is that I come on bended knee. I stand here praying, hoping, promising that my next go-around on this old globe might be one that draws me closer to the unfettered essence I was meant to be. The one not weighted down with doubt and double-guessing. The one that drinks in all the holy waters all around me.

Dorothy [Day, activist, writer, and cofounder of the Catholic Worker movement] devoted an entire book to Thérèse of Lisieux and her spirituality of "the little way." St. Thérèse indicated the path to holiness that lay within all our daily occupations. Simply, it consisted of performing, in the presence and love of God, all the little things that make up our everyday life and contact with others. From Thérèse, Dorothy learned that any act of love might contribute to the balance of love in the world, any suffering endured in love might ease the burden of others; such was the mysterious bond within the Body of Christ. We could only make use of the little things we possessed—the little faith, the little strength, the little courage. These were the loaves and fishes. We could only offer what we had, and pray that God would make the increase. It was all a matter of faith.[1]

It is, I hope and pray and believe, by little and by little—by little dose of courage, by little kindness, by little gentleness—that we inhale the promise: to shake off our wobbles, stand tall, and launch the climb again.

Sometimes, often, it takes time—and stumbling and skinning our knees and getting back up again—till we figure out what's most essential, maybe most obvious.

The more I read, the more I listen, the more deeply I understand that the miracle we're after, the wonder we seek, the beauty that tingles our spine—it doesn't come with timpani, but rather in the accumulated whisper of one small blessing after another. The blessings at once unadorned and majestic. The blessings that make us whole and fill us when we're hollowed.

Prayer for the Children

My prayer at the dawn of this day is for the children.

I think in particular of a deep-eyed girl of seven who lives in faraway Maine, a little girl who holed herself in her chandelier-lit bedroom the other day, listening all day to the speeches of Martin Luther King Jr., a little girl who asks questions about how to use her voice—to speak out when she hears a girl teasing her friend on the playground, to speak up for what she believes, without fear that she'll wind up unloved and pushed aside in the process.

She's a little girl who is finding her way through the tangled landscape of fairness and justice, who is looking to the grown-ups around her to find the tools she'll make her own, the tools that just might allow her to leave this world a little bit more whole—and more healed—than when she arrived.

My prayer is for that little girl. My prayer is for all the children, the ones waking up, perhaps, on a wobbly cot, under a thin blanket, squeezed tight against the mama who protects them from unthinkable things in the night. I am thinking, too, of the children who wake up not far from me, in bedrooms where walls are covered in papers and paints that cost more per square foot or per gallon than some of us could ever fathom.

I pray for them all.

Because children don't get a say in where they are born, and in whose arms they find themselves cradled. They don't choose who soothes them; they ask only to be soothed, and fed, and kept warm and kept dry. They beg to be loved.

If they're blessed, they're anointed with all of those things. If there are eyes to gaze back at them, a voice to whisper—or sing—to them, if there are arms to scoop them up when they cry, well, then they've already won the baby lottery.

Children are pure at birth, and not yet thick-skinned. They're nearly translucent, in matters of heart and soul anyway. Their job early on is to pay close attention, the attention of saints and prophets. They're keeping watch in hopes of figuring out just who it is they want to be, and how they might best find their own circuitous way through the wilds.

I pray for them this newborn morning because I want theirs to be a world where goodness and kindness and gentleness seep in, seep to their core, bathe them through and through in truth and justice and love in purest tincture.

I want the grown-ups around them, and even the ones far away, to commit, day after day, to trying to show them these few fine things: tenderness, honesty, strength of courage, and moral resolve. I want them enveloped in the very strands at the core of every sacred text ever inscribed.

I want children to be able to tune into the world beyond their front doors and not hear vitriol, not see ugliness. I want them to listen to sharp and curious minds engaged in debate and dialogue, free from jagged edge, free from acid-tinged tone. I pray to God they don't some day aimlessly change the channel and stumble on images of war-pummeled children, images of children covered in dust and rubble and blood from their wounds, children dumped—or washed ashore—lifeless. I pray most mightily for that reel of terrible images—and the wars from which they're captured—to come to an end, that no children suffer those terrible ends. I pray that children no longer know terror.

I want children, all children, to hear the booming voice of hope, of words that lift the human spirit and set it soaring. I want them to feel wrapped in a message that tingles their spine, because even a child—especially a child—knows beautiful when she or he hears it.

I want each child to know full well that he or she can dream wildly, can be the very someone he or she chooses and works to be. I don't want children to know the sound of a door slamming in their faces, or the screech of a siren carrying them—or someone they dearly love—far, far away. I don't want a single child to be scared to death, to be breathless with fear. I don't want hands and arms ripped away from them. I don't want a child left alone in a classroom or closet or train car, left cowering in a corner.

I want for these children the world and the country that I believe in—one that looks much like the world as God first imagined it: skin in a thousand shades of brown and black and cream and bronze. I want a melting pot where everyone gets a fair and solid chance. I want books—gloriously written tomes—to be as close as the nearest library. I want teachers to fill classrooms where learning is rich and intellects are lit on fire. I want leaders with backbone, with the courage to stand up and say, "That's not right, that's a lie, that's unfair, or unjust, or just plain hateful."

I want a sky that's uncluttered with smog and poisonous fumes. I want a child to be able to poke his or her head out the window at night and count the stars, connect the dots of heaven's light, name the constellations. I want the rivers and streams to gurgle and babble and rush and roar. I want children to know the sound of a leaf crunching underfoot, or even a wee little creature scampering by— close enough, perhaps, to muster a fright, an innocent fright, the fright of the woods.

I want children to sit down to a table where there's food from the earth, wholesome food, unsullied food. Food to make the child whole, and strong, and able.

I want children to be strong of body and sinew and bone, yet I know that can't always be. And for those who are not—not strong, and not able, for children who are sick, or born with terrible burdens—I want them to be able to find a doctor or nurse or health-care worker who can get to the bottom of the mystery, the quandary, the illness, and work toward a cure. Or at least erase the suffering, as much as is humanly possible. I'll beg God to step in to take care of all the rest, and to ease the worries too—of mama and papa and child, and anyone else who lies awake fretting every dreaded what-if.

I want for all the world's children all the very same things I want for my own: I want them to know deeply that they are loved. I want them to know there is a heart always willing to listen, to hear every last utterance of their worries or fears or confusions. I want them to know that all around there are great good souls who are gentle and kind and unceasingly fair, souls who do not reach for words as weapons of hurt, or of hate.

I want them to know: when I've run out of answers, when I cannot quell the trembles, or chase away the darkness, there is a God who's always in reach.

I want their prayers to be answered, and mine to be heard.

And I promise, with all my heart on this day, to do all I can to make certain the world I imagine, the world that I want, is the one I work hard to make come true. I'll do my part. Starting right now. As the sun rises, again.

A Prayer to Be Our Best Selves

When we sat down to dinner the other night, we clasped hands as we always do, maybe a little tighter that night than we sometimes do, and we nodded toward the gentle man at the far end of the table, the man whose moral ballast, whose capacities to anchor my fevered flights, weighed deeply into why I married him. It was his turn to say the prayer. He spoke simply, two sentences perhaps. And the one that's stuck with me all week, the one I've all but sewn to my backbone, to put muscle to my wobbly self, is this:

"Dear God, let us be our best selves."

It's as wise an instruction as any I've stumbled upon this week.

What it means, I think, is to double down on our inclinations to be living-breathing beacons of all that's good. And by *good* we mean those actions inscribed in every ancient and timeless holy text: love as you would be loved. Turn the other cheek. Be your brother's or your sister's keeper.

To name a few (please, name a few that guide you) . . .

When the world around you feels as if the ground's been shaken, when you're scared by all the words (and acts) of hate that swirl around, is there any hope in muscling on more deeply attuned to your own code of gentle kindness, in reaching across the darkness in search of the glimmering shard of holiness we're sure is somewhere out there?

Is there any other choice?

Some Thoughts on the Cradle That Is Prayer

*P*rayer, on my good days, is how I breathe. It's listening, as much as whispering. It takes the wobble out of my knees and puts the wallop into my heart's beat. It's woven into the hours, from cock's crow until the moment my eyelids finally flutter closed for the day. It unspools without measure or meter. It might be a geyser. Or merely a murmur.

The other morning, when I was deep in meditation, it came to me that prayer, at its holiest, is a cradle, woven from filaments of wonder and wisdom. Prayer, at its most powerful, perhaps, as transitive verb. Picture yourself swept into arms that hold you, that rock you, that lull you. Prayer, cradling.

Cradle, my dictionary tells me, is "to hold something gently and protectively." Etymologists, those learned folk who poke around in the vaults of centuries past for linguistic DNA, tell me the word has thirteenth-century Old English roots and trace its cognates to Old

High German *kratto, krezzo,* "basket"; and German *Krätze,* "basket carried on the back."

In the sixteenth century, the noun slipped into its form as a verb, and that's how I like it best. To be cradled. To cradle.

Isn't "to be cradled" to be rocked into sleepy-eyed quietude, to be harbored against harsh winds? Is that not a root of prayer?

And so I am—we are all—being cradled. Each and every day. Even—especially—the days when breathing comes shallow and rapid and hard, even the days when we're mostly holding our breath. We are cradled in great, tender arms that enwrap us. I particularly love the notion from the German *Krätze,* "basket carried on the back." Breathe that one in for a moment.

Might we be the basket carried on God's back? Might our cares, our worries, our rubbed-raw heartaches be hoisted onto shoulders far mightier than our own? "Basket carried on the back." Prayer, cradled.

Cradled is but one of prayer's verbs. Prayer plays out in a symphony of verbs. Many, many verbs. I've come to believe, over time and across the arc of keeping watch, in prayer of the transitive and intransitive ilk. Prayer in motion. Prayer put to muscle. Or imagination. Or heart. Prayer that deepens us, draws us to our core.

Never more so than motherprayer, a matrix of prayer in all its iterations that animates my every breath, most every rippled thought, and, more often than not, keeps me from plunging overboard.

My prayer today might cradle me. And it might come in the simple act of pressing cheek-to-cheek against my sleeping boy, a prayer of gratitude if ever there was. My prayer might come in counting stars, a prayer of wonder, always. For me, it's all a hodgepodge, no single stream of prayerfulness. No exacting measure. I simply know it's prayer when, as so often happens, I feel the mighty hand of God sprinkle goose bumps down my arms. When my leaden heart is lifted. When the door to the impossible is at long last unlocked, and hope comes rushing in.

The dilemma, though, is this: we live in a world where, too often, prayer—in any form—feels out of reach. Some of us don't have an inkling where or how to begin. The few lines we know, the ones we might have memorized a long, long time ago, fall flat. Miss the mark. And what about the hours when words won't come at all, when language escapes us? When we're enveloped by a hollow silence without end? It's suffocating emptiness, hopelessness defined.

Here, then, is a lifeline: we needn't find our way to the topography of prayer through words alone. In fact, sometimes, I think, we get tangled in the words, and the truest unfettered prayer is the prayer that catapults beyond scripted lines. How will I move into uncharted nooks and crannies of my soul if I merely grope along clinging hard and stubbornly to words?

Words uncork welled-up parts of me, deep inside. Words put wings to my heart and soul, take me soaring. Words move me to tears.

Words have been known to crumple me. I might spend the better part of an afternoon contemplating a single string of words, ones deliberately lobbed my way or merely snatched in passing. I daydream words. Pin them side by side, affix them as frilly French knots to plainspoken cross-stitched sentences, behold them for their singular capacity to take my breath away or merely tickle one of my fancies.

And yet, the undeniable truth, sad as it is, is that words—no matter how hard we try—can carry us only so far. And the destination I seek in prayer is one that lies far beyond the boundaries of language.

I've a hunch, a fairly certain one, that the native landscape of prayer—prayer at its deepest—is the one that sprawls on the far side of the chockablock of words. And once there, it's without boundary.

Prayer, if we pay attention, if we deepen, breaks out of linguistic binds. Takes flight. Bores deep. It's free-form verse. As near as our next breath. I've come to believe that prayer—the prayer I love best—is the practice of paying attention.

I can't help thinking of St. Francis of Assisi, who, according to oft-repeated but never-nailed-down legend, is said to have instructed his followers: preach the gospel at all times—if necessary, use words.

Prayer might come in the act of tending a garden. Or keeping watch on the wilderness from high atop the forest ranger's lookout tower. Prayer, I've found, is what a farmer does when she genuflects amid the soybean rows and rattles away the hungry Japanese beetle. Prayer unfurls in soprano, offered up at the deathbed at the hour of someone's final breath. Prayer is what fills the heart as the midwife reaches for the newborn's crowning head and eases him into the holy light of delivery. Prayer, for me, is most often born of mothering.

Perhaps you already believe, as I do, that prayer is the hundred thousand little acts of kindness, of hope, of selflessness we stitch into the day. It's stirring porridge on a cold winter's morning for those we love, still nestled in beds. Delivering a piping-hot casserole, or a store-bought cake, to a lonely neighbor. Prayer is tucking a little one into bed. Talking over the long, hard day at the kitchen counter. Prayer is rolling up your sleeves and scrubbing a sick friend's bathroom floor. Prayer is at its glorious best when we soar beyond words. It's what we do and how we breathe.

Sometimes, when I'm perched at the rocky edge, teetering toward the vast, inky pit that is despair at its darkest, or sadness or worry in gradations of gray, I lean into the one of which I'm sure: God. I take a lung-filling breath and rest against what I know to be tender and solid and always there—once I quiet the noise of my own making, that is. I begin, sometimes, with two simple words: "Take this." Or, maybe, "You there?" Then, as my breathing slows, I feel as if a hand is pressed against the small of my back, as if my shoulders are blanketed. I'm steadied. I'm filling—with hope and holy whisper. It's the whisper of God, gently tapping me upside the noggin and deep in the heart, reminding: *I'm here, right here. And I'm not leaving.*

Perhaps you, too, subscribe to the notion that prayer needs no words. That prayer sometimes is simply breathing. It is inhabiting the holy sphere where we know we're bathed in purest light. Where, as with a dear, dear soul mate, we can sit side by side, wrapped in silence.

Prayer, a wise priest once told me, is practicing the presence of God.

The prayer I pray most deeply, most often, is my unending loop of motherprayer.

A Few Thoughts on the Particulars of Motherprayer

*I*t is what we do on days like this. We worry, yes. We scramble eggs. We pack lunches, thick with steak. We check on bedroom lights late into the night. Make sure they're off and tousled heads are sleeping. We drive. Deliver children to the schoolhouse door. And all day long, we keep an eye on clocks.

Short of picking up a pencil, slip-sliding into a school desk, and making like we're the ones who know the path to truth on the exam, we really haven't many worldly options. Not in test-taking season. Nor any other season that makes the growing-up years a labyrinth that's laced with snap-traps and chutes and tippity ladders.

And so, we surrender.

We employ the mother tongue as ancient as any known. Since first birth (and I mean the dawn of time), I'd wager, there have been mothers who turn their words, their breath, their whispered vespers to the ineffable, the uncharted, the place where hope plays hide-and-seek.

We pray.

We fill in the blanks with supplications that wash out from deep inside us, and over us, and far into the beyond.

We pray for hours if we have to, keeping on with all the rest we do. Not letting on that there is prayer at work.

We drop to knees. We dab holy water, head and chest and shoulders, the sign of the cross. We lie down and stretch our arms as high as we can reach. We venerate. We call on God, and ones we love who are no longer but might well come to the holy blessed rescue.

Oh, yes.

I've seen heavyhearted mothers, on their knees, crawl up great stone church steps and inch their way down a long, long aisle that ripped their flesh but not their spirit, dead set they were on laying down their knotted, bundled prayers at the foot of a bare and marbled altar.

I've heard mothers ululate, sending untamed sounds to a place that understands, even if we've no idea just where that someplace is.

We pray, we mothers all, in many creeds and faiths and dialects, but always in one united tongue: we pray for our children.

We pray for what they need. We pray for what's beyond our reach, but so help us, we'll provide—if prayer can make it be.

There is an alchemy to prayer. A mysticism that cannot be explained. It is holy pleading raised to the nth power.

Motherprayer needn't be explained.

We wrap our children, their whole life long, in motherprayer. And motherprayer is infinite and lasts forever.

Motherprayer picks up where earthly mother cannot reach.

Motherprayer is wholly holy. And holiness has ears, I've learned, for all that's spilled in never-ending prayer of mother.

You pray, and you pray mightily. You get down on your knees. You beg at the locked gate of heaven. You make deals, if you have to. And you pray to God that you do not hear only the echo of your deep incantation lost in the canyon of No.

And the Child's Prayer

(These words, tragically, were written in the wake of the heart-shattering news that a shooter, armed with a gun called a Glock, had sprayed bullets into a crowd outside a supermarket in Tucson, Arizona; one of those bullets pierced the heart of a nine-year-old, another forever maimed a United States congresswoman.)

It was last Friday night, I am nearly certain, when my little one, who sometimes is a prophet, climbed into our bed. He wanted snuggles, he said. And then, as he was wrapped from both sides by arms that have harbored him since that long-ago hot August night when his eight whopping pounds first slipped upon us, he spoke the words that have blanketed me all week:

"I like when you hug me. I feel like the whole world is around me, and I feel like nothing could ever hurt me."

It's not every night you find yourself wrapped around poetry.

"I like when you hug me. I feel like the whole world is around me, and I feel like nothing could ever hurt me."

So we hold our breath and pray.

So we wish.

So we fool ourselves every time we wrap our arms around the ones we love.

As if it's a shield that cannot be shattered. As if impenetrable walls are forever wrapped around the ones we love, the vulnerable ones, the ones who do not—do not—have rhyme or reason to be taken away.

Lord, have mercy.

My little boy's words, now a refrain I tumble round my brain, like some succulent fruit whose juice I cannot get enough of, his words are what we pray for.

His words are what we need to remember.

Isn't that the prayer at the heart of all our comings and goings?

"I like when you hug me. I feel like the whole world is around me, and I feel like nothing could ever hurt me."

It is all our children ask of us, in the end, to be their shields from the darkness, to chase away the ghosts and goblins, the creaks in the hall in the thick of the night, the ones that scare them to no end.

They lean their little bodies into us, into our soft chests. They ask for so little: *Wrap me, make me feel safe, shoosh away the monsters.*

And while there might always be madmen, and madwomen, who steal the light, who shatter the morning's hope, our jobs do not cease.

Our arms are forever needed, and the hearts that beat in the middle:

"I like when you hug me. I feel like the whole world is around me, and I feel like nothing could ever hurt me."

It just might be our most important job: hug the ones you love today. Pray with all your might that you can keep them safe—from harm, from hurt, from monsters.

On a Mother's Courage

Motherhood is always an act of courage."

I think of the mothers I admire most, the ones whose unbroken, unwobbling faith makes me stand straight, breathe deep, reach down, and get a grip. I think of those mothers and realize every single one is a profile in pure courage.

We lift our voices, if need be. Make decisions. Stand taller than we've ever stood. Because it is our children for whom we are called to be more than we have ever been before.

It is courage—the hot wind of heaven that fuels our trembling wings.

It is courage—that makes us reach down deep and pull out muscle where we never knew we had it. It's where the backbone is. It's where, when we need to, we find the voice that speaks up, that won't relent, that settles only in solid resolution.

We are charged with much in this lifelong journey called mothering.

The one piece of armament sure to go the distance is the unfettered, unadorned, magnificent holy breath called Mother Courage.

And she comes to me through prayer, and prayer alone.

On Motherlove

I began to contemplate how love, especially motherlove, is the sum of infinites. Minute, and barely perceptible, although wholly definable and defining, they are the accumulated brushstrokes and palm presses and finger squeezes that imprint, somehow, on the souls of those whose care—whose fevered limbs, swollen glands, fractured bones, woopsy tummies—we cradle.

It is through the sum of infinitely loving, and infinite signature touches, that the little ones whose flesh and blood and coos and cries we were handed not so long ago will grow up wholly defining how it is to be ministered to, to be loved, to be—yes—mothered, no matter who the motherer.

And thus our unmeasurable infinite acts will go forth into infinity. A mighty sum—born, simply, out of love.

The New-Year Kitchen

*A*s the curtain rises on the newborn year, we find ourselves tucking away tins, now emptied of all but the last sweet crumbs, vestige of merriment, of splurge upon splurge. Hibernation—an old-fashioned word for *hygge* (that *au courant* Danish term for "cozy comforts")—beckons. Which might be why depth of winter is the season that draws me closest to the cookstove. I practically purr puttering around the kitchen. All-day pots bubble away, lulling me into dreamy meditative fugues. Slow cooking, I'd wager, was made for snowy days, stay-inside days. Doughs rise. Wine-steeped stews simmer. Chowders thicken. Fruity compotes collapse into jewel-toned ooze. It's all a plethora of stove-top seduction, as what you pitch into the pot gives way, a few hours in, to heat and spice and saintly patience. It's kitchen adagio, the slow dance of surrender. And at the cookstove, trophies come dolloped on fork or soupspoon. Either way, you won't want to dash too soon.

Worth-the-Wait Porridge

When your morning prayer on a particular day—a day that demands much, too much, from its players—seems most aptly punctuated by the stirring of spoon through a muddle of oats. When the first thing you reach for, come dawn, is the grain that amounts to a mother's amulet. And as you stand there tossing in handfuls of shriveled-up gems—fruits the colors of amethyst, ruby, garnet, or onyx—you imagine yourself some sort of sorceress, arming your brood for the slaying of dragons to come.

Provenance: Nigel Slater + Felicity Cloake + *The Ballymaloe Cookbook*

Yield: 2 bowls, or 1 if you find yourself famished after a long night's nap

> 1 cup rolled or steel-cut oats*
> 3 cups water**
> ¼ teaspoon salt
> Assorted accoutrements: dried cranberries, apricots, raisins; sliced banana, chunks of apple; handfuls of almonds or walnuts; a spoon of peanut or almond butter; a sprinkling of wheat germ; a drizzle of honey or molasses; a spoonful of brown sugar. (Any of these would likely leave a porridge purist aghast, but some mornings a bit of rabble-rousing *is* the order of the day.)

* Porridge *cognoscenti* all prescribe Flahavan's Irish Porridge Oats, if you're aiming for indescribable deliciousness.
** While water is traditional—in fact, *The Scots Kitchen,*

F. Marian McNeill's recently republished 1929 classic, recommends spring water—porridge is sometimes made with hot milk, although that might mark you as a sybarite.

After culling dozens of porridge recipes, I've determined that all the enlightened porridgers subscribe to a quick toasting of the oats, a mere minute or two in a dry porridge pot over medium heat, until faintly golden. (If you choose steel-cut oats or a mix of rolled and steel-cut, you'll want to soak the steel-cut bits overnight, pouring boiling water in three-to-one ratio, water to oats, atop the oats and parking them off in the corner. Put the lid on the pot, and bid them goodnight.)

Next morning, or when your belly's growling for that proper porridge, add water to oats in the pot (unless you've gone for the overnight soak), or if you prefer your oats creamier, make it milk or even cream. Whichever your pleasure, keep to that three-to-one fluid-to-oats ratio, your golden ratio here. (If you've opted for the all-night immersion, you might need to add just a glug of water or milk in the morning so your oatsy bits are sufficiently aswim. But after a long night's idle, your steel-cut bits likely will need little but heat at this point. And fret not: oats might be the original forgiving grain.)

Stir, on low heat. A good five to ten minutes, please. Yes, stirring without pause—long, slow, meditative circles with your wooden spoon, or spurtle, a flat wooden stirring utensil designed by the Scots in the fifteenth century to keep oats from going lumpy, but of course. (Opines Mr. Slater: "Stirring is essential if the porridge is to be truly creamy.")

Add salt after porridge has been cooking for a good five to ten minutes. (Again, notes Nigel: "If the salt is introduced too early, it can harden the oats. Porridge needs cooking for longer than you think if the starch is to be fully cooked.")

Put the lid on your porridge pot and remove from the heat. Allow the velvety mound to breathe deeply and surrender to its steamy confines. A five-minute rest at a minimum. There is simply no hurrying a porridge of proper production.

Ladle into your favorite bowl, douse with a splash of fresh, cold milk, and adorn with handfuls of whatever accoutrements brighten your morning. Or to put it as the British food scribe Felicity Cloake so poetically puts it in *The Guardian* of London (and why wouldn't you want to put it thusly?): "A girdle of very cold milk, or single cream on special occasions, is essential . . . but a knob of butter, while melting attractively into the oats, proves too greasy for my taste."

Springtime

Season of Quickening

*I*n the weeks and months ahead, we are wise to find sacred lessons in earth's awakening, in the sloughing off of winter's harshest blows. With every passing day, we're drawn deeper and deeper into the palpitations of springtime: its heartbreak, its births and rebirths, its many deaths, its rising from darkness. Tender is all around; so too, resilience. Even the world's religions pause for vernal truths as resurrection and exodus are themes of the stories told and retold in Eastertide and Passover. The leitmotifs of liturgical spring: rebirth, triumph over trial, hope rising again. Springtime pushes us to the sharp edge of the season's turning, insists we stay alert, not sleep through holy hours. In the realm of mothering, the syllabus of spring is rich in blessed instruction: pay attention, close attention, keep close watch, for all of this will be whisked away before the next breeze ceases its blowing. And never extinguish hope.

Springtime's Wonderlist

it's the season of . . .

fiddleheads, furled and heaped in balsa-wood crates, a tumult of tight-wound woodland commas . . .

unheralded—and short-breathed—warmth, carried in on southerly winds, chased off just as suddenly by insistent northerlies . . .

nest making, dialed up by the hour, as the hatching days draw near . . .

windows shoved ajar—at last and hallelujah—because you cannot stand to keep out that resurrecting vernal air . . .

crushing snowfall, and it's your heart that's crushed as the mounds flatten newly trumpeting daffodils . . .

serendipitous picnic on the lakeshore's chilly sands . . .

softening afternoons, epilogue to blanket-burrowing dawn . . .

puddles primed for rubber boots . . .

scribble your own springtime wonders here . . .

A Count-Your-Blessings Calendar

Blessed Be Springtime, Season of Quickening

VERNAL EQUINOX: Glory be spring, season of exodus and resurrection, of life unfurling, but, too, life tumbling from the nest. Or, sadder yet, getting pushed. It's death and life all over. To be reborn, the preachers shout, you first must die.

BLESSING 2: The whole top half of the world is shaking off its winter death. But death is the necessary somber note in the song of spring. Hand in hand with life. This is the season of light and shadow. And why it takes our breath away.

BLESSING 3: The Japanese, enlightened, teach that the beauty of the cherry blossom is its evanescence. The very fact that at any minute a breeze might blow and blossoms will be scattered. Theirs is a deep understanding of the season's essence. They're keen to what it's teaching: Behold the blossom. It won't last for long.

BLESSING 4: Pay attention to the barely perceptible growth of early spring. The first sprouts at the branch's far end, practically poking you in the eye, announcing, "Hey, look, I'm not just a stick anymore." Comb the earth, hike the woods. Get down on your knees, if you must. We, too, grow in barely perceptible bits. Sometimes it doesn't take much, just the barest measure of growing, of quarter-inching toward life, to make all the difference.

BLESSING 5: If you find a baby bird fallen from the nest to its death, whisper a proper benediction as you perform a proper burial. Lay a sprig of springtime flowers. Teach a child to do the same.

EASTERTIDE: Salute the day-after-day resurrection of the sunrise: Awake before the dawn, amble out to where you can catch the hoisting up of the fiery orb, stretch before its first-cast sunbeams, bow down, be humbled. Remember that God is light eternal.

BLESSING 7: The Italians have a word tristesse. "Beautiful sorrow," I was told it meant. Knowing that what you love won't last. And so you love more deeply. Is this the truth of spring?

BLESSING 8: It's seesaw season, yin and yang. It's stripping off old skin, it's starting over. It's tender and it's green, beginning green. Everything feels tender all over. Even us, some days. Be kind to your tender spots—they just might be where essential truths seep in.

APRIL FOOL'S DAY (APRIL 1): Crouch down, inspect the growing things. Take note of miracles that unfold in dark of night and light of day when we're not looking, hunched inside, distracted by too-long lists of things we tell ourselves we must do. But must we, really?

BLESSING 10: Tiptoe outdoors once twilight deepens into darkness. Read the night sky. When you spy a twinkling star, whisper a prayer of infinite thanks for heaven's lamplights.

MAY DAY (MAY 1): Caretaker of Wonder Pledge: I will rescue broken flowers and ferry them to my windowsill infirmary, where I'll apply remedies and potions, or simply watch them fade away in peace.

MOTHERING DAY (SECOND SUNDAY IN MAY): Tutorial in patience: Mama bird constructing her nest, one blade of grass after another. Note how she shops for just the right twig, sizing up then promptly ditching the stick that will not do. Study the ingenious troves where she gathers snips of string. We should all be so intent on our tasks.

BLESSING 13: Try not to be crushed in these hold-your-breath weeks when, say, your heirloom hyacinth is just beginning to bat its smoky-lavender lashes, and you wake up to find the opossums had a hoedown, broke the stalk in two. As you scoop up the remains, tuck the bloom in water, whisper a prayer, contemplate the ways you might revive your own broken dreams.

BLESSING 14: Bless the wildflowers, who even now, are plotting where to rise up from the summer's meadow, and who will sway beside whom. You might stroll through the nearest clearing, where first tips of green are poking through the earth, letting you in on the next season's stitchwork sampler.

Awakening Stirrings

*I*t's all new-born right now. The leaves, just beginning their term, as if cut from a fat bolt of velvet, pinned onto branches, by the night seamstress, the sorceress of spring, who wisps through the dark delighting our senses, making way for the morning show, when the curtain of dawn rises.

Everywhere, the earth is shouting: *Wake up, you sleepyheads. Wipe the goop from your eyes, slip on your galoshes, and come give it a gander.*

Just yesterday, someone asked me how I find the way to slow time, how I set my own internal clock to a rhythm that allows the sacred to seep in.

"Well, it begins with the dawn," I said. It begins when I'm all alone, just me and God and the birth of another blessed day. (Truth be told, I still miss my fat old cat, the furry acolyte who met me at the door, who rubbed his ears against my ankles, followed me to the prayer bench where I often plop on days that don't insist on abbreviated vespers. The old fellow literally curled up and died a few weeks back, and the morning's been hollowed ever since.)

Once I've inhaled deeply of the dawn, once I've filled my ears with the song of the feathered choristers, watched the flocks swoop in for their fill of what I've dumped from my old banged-up coffee can, once I've watched the curled-up buds on all the boughs, taken measure of their proximity to blossoming, I lay down an undercoat of prayer. I name the ones for whom the blessings are most urgent. I name the ones I love, one by one, as if the mere pronunciation of their name is an anointing. And then I press those prayers into place through the simple act of breathing. Isn't prayer sometimes simply intermingling earthly breath with the breath of the Divine, heaven's reach swirling down to lift us from our leaden station? Isn't prayer the posture that takes away what weighs us down, that shares the yoke? That wraps us in the hold that whispers, "You're not alone. This isn't yours to carry all by your weary, worn-out self."

It's the holy hour that pulls me from my bed. The one certain anchor to begin another day. The grace of dawn is my beginning. As if a golden-threaded vestment into which I slip my arms, it's the only wrap I know that holds the hope of peace throughout the hours still to come.

Here we are, back in the part where, if we're paying attention, we find ourselves in the minute-by-minute explosion of all that's been quietly waiting out the winter. It's slow seduction, this day by day, hour by hour, unfurling of all that's within. Mama Earth doesn't give away all her hallelujahs at once. She wants you back, she wants you keeping close watch on her show, so she lures you in, a slo-mo unveiling of all of her secrets.

There's divine wisdom, indeed, in this once-a-year whirl through the explosion of spring. The earth is literally bursting with the beautiful. It's beckoning, begging: *Crouch down, pay attention. Give a sniff. Plop your bum. Inhale. Watch me unfurl. I'll give you a wallop, minute by minute.*

In a thousand million mind-spinning ways the whole of creation is clued in to the infinite wisdom: this is your gift; it's yours for the taking. All you need do is open your eyes, open your ears and your nose, pry open your heart—and your soul while you're at it—and let in the holiest whisper.

It's the wake-up call of heaven and earth.

The springs of our lifetime are numbered, and they won't last forever and ever. The beauty is now. Go bury your nose in the whole of it.

And whisper a fine hallelujah.

Instruction for Springtime (And, Truly, All the Seasons Beyond)

I will teach my children to look and look closely. I will teach them the glory of God is there through the lens. But they must open their hearts, as well as their eyes, to soak in the sights. To regard. To watch. To take in the world. It is the often unnoticed to which I must teach them to pay the closest attention.

"You must do something to make the world more beautiful."

So instructs Miss Rumphius, the protagonist of the children's book that vies for most-blessed on my shelf. Close as a children's book comes to gospel, far as I'm concerned.

Miss Rumphius, the real-life great aunt of Barbara Cooney, the great children's book writer and illustrator, is little and old when we meet her on the very first page of the very fine book. She lives in a little house overlooking the sea, on an island in Maine. But she hadn't always been old, we are told. She had been young, and she dreamed, and she longed to travel the world. When she was young, she spent her days by her grandpapa's side in his wood-carving shop, where he chiseled away at great chunks of trees, making them into curlicues and cherubs and figureheads for the prows of great sailing ships, ships that would crisscross the seas. And, sometimes, when her grandpapa got too busy to finish his paintings of sailing ships and faraway places, he would let little Alice (for that was her name before she was called Miss Rumphius) pick up his paint brush and "put in the skies" of his paintings. And in the evenings, when she sat on her grandpapa's lap, curled up for the great and nearly lost art of unspooling stories, she told him she too wanted to sail the world like those ships and, someday, live beside the sea. Her grandpapa said that was all well and good, but there was a third thing she must do: "You must do something to make the world more beautiful."[1]

It's an instruction that's ancient and timeless, and new every day.

Tender Is the Earth: A Call to Surrender

I am submitting to the tilting of the earth. As the oozy patch of mud that is my very own fraction of acreage leans into the less-diluted rays of the great burning star that is the sun, pivot point of the universe, as adagio quickens, and feathered choristers raise their warbles by decibels upon decibels, I allow myself to be wrapped in the soft skeins of earth unfurling, earth letting loose its tight and clenched long-winter's grip.

I am brushing up against its tendrils, its newborn threads, as I tiptoe down my bluestone walk. As I plop my bum on bluestone stoop, the one that hasn't yet released its wintry chill, I crouch down low, and run my fingertips across the frilly tops of fronds, just beginning to poke beyond the crust of earth, just beginning to contemplate the art of opening, sun salutation of the new spring garden.

I can't get close enough—save for rolling in the dewy grass, smearing fists of mud across my knees and elbows. Or climbing up a tree, to discover how it feels to be a bird, warbling across the heavens, toes clinging to the bough.

All in all, my daily pull is to the pulse point where earth and sky entwine, where winter's hibernation gives way to springtime's insistent release. I drink in the lessons, the unspoken parable: it's letting-go time, it's time to uncoil, time to put aside the winter pose—one born of sorrow, yes, and a hollowed-out sense of quietude—time to practice the gentle nudge, bow down low to the invitation, the one that whispers, "I offer healing, if you lean in close, breathe deep the wholeness, the promise, of the season."

I allow myself, day upon day, hour after hour, to be soothed by the blessed balm of earth at its tenderest. Of earth when heaven first begins to draw forth what's been tucked inside for all the weeks and months of darkness.

Those Fine Few Things We Teach Our Children, All Along the Way

On Teaching Tenderness

"It's worm-rescue weather," I told my little one, stepping out the door and over the rivulet running east along the stoop. "This is when the worms come out, thinking they'll just grab a little gulp of rain. But then, sometimes, the rains dry up and the poor worms are stranded there on all the sidewalks."

I leapt right in, waited not for him to play along. Or even sign a waiver of intent.

"Here wormy, wormy, wormy," I called, scanning here and there for a waylaid invertebrate, a worm who'd lost its way, a worm, by golly, who'd had far too much to drink and could not slither home. Or just had given in to wormly je ne sais quoi. Ennui, perhaps, of the earthworm ilk. Up and called it quits in the middle of a concrete wasteland.

The little one—too young to drop me by the hand and sprint, too old to merely play along—interrupted.

"Hey, Mom, I don't think that's gonna work," he said. "I think that just works for a cat or a dog. But then you have to say their name, the cat's name or the dog's name. Doggy, doggy doesn't work. And wormy, wormy doesn't either."

Oh.

He had a point, but I had little option. No worms I knew had names. Or not that I'd been told.

It took three more blocks of worm patrol before, at last, we found a spineless wonder stranded on the walk.

It had inches to go before it made it back to dirt and grass, where it stood a chance of escaping errant tricycles or big, flat soles that paid no mind to where they landed.

As I knelt down to teach the tender art of lifting on a stick and plopping the straggler onto the grass, my trusty sidekick kicked in, all right.

"Oh, worm," he started in, "just to tell you, you're disgusting." And then to robin on a limb: "Oh, robin, here's a worm."

It is slow teaching, this curriculum of tenderness toward all things living, and even those that aren't.

On Life-and-Death Curriculum

We often think the long nights we've spent on bathroom floors with a retching or fevered child, the midnight hours when we're the ones knocking ice cubes from the freezer, we think of those, sometimes, as invisible hours, times that draw no notice. What we might not realize is that in that transactional moment, when ice practically sizzles on a fevered brow, when a kid so sick he can barely open his droopy lids lets us slip an ice chip to his tongue, what we're doing is so much more than knocking back a fever. We are quietly, and without folderol, teaching something sacred to the essence of being human. Maybe fevers and flus were invented for the simple purpose of one someone being invited to try to heal another.

A life-and-death curriculum is unfurling here in the quiet of our humdrum little lives. Our whole life long we are teaching and learning that most magnificent of golden rules: love as you would be loved.

On Mercy, Learned

(Upon finding a robin's nest thrashed to the ground after a pelting all-night's rain. A perfect robin's nest, mud-daubed, for stability; tucked within with fine, soft grasses, upholstery for eggs. Coming upon it, you see two eggs, perfect ovoid realms of possibility, but a third is cracked and oozing. A baby bird inside, its heart no longer beating. And mama bird, nowhere in sight. You lift the fallen nursery from the sodden grass, hold it high, an offering, a benediction . . .)

In my mama's book of rules, you do not leave a sacred something lying there abandoned. As if a discard. There are no discards when it comes to nature. Only lessons to be learned. And mercy studied.

Night Prayer

Shabbat had tiptoed in, as it always does, praise be to God who promised it.

Prayers would begin any minute at the church, yes, where our synagogue dwells. The cantor would lift up a minor-key chord, the rabbi would open the book. And all of us, the few of us, gathered there would begin.

Only this Friday night I wouldn't be there.

I knew, deep in the place that knows all these things, that a room with walls and a roof, even a room with windows taller and wider than I'll ever be, wasn't big enough for my prayers. Not this Friday night.

So, while the man who I love went to pray in that room, I went to the edge of the lake. I went to where the trees reach into the night, finger the darkness. Where the dome scrapes the edge of infinity. Where no prayer is too big.

I went to the place where, uncannily, eerily, that night, the lake made no sound. Not a whimper of wave. Nothing but stillness.

Then, from out of the black, out of the dense, deep thickness that is night at the beach, I heard the lone cry of a night-flying goose. I couldn't make out its wings, couldn't see a wisp of its shadow.

All I know is I heard it, high overhead. Calling and crying and breaking the night with a sorrowful mourning song, not unlike the one in my soul.

I sat there, on the sand in the cold, looking up into the moonless night. Not even the moon made itself known that dark night at the edge of the lake.

Somewhere, though, I knew, it was out there, the moon, round and white, absorbing, reflecting, the light of the number one star. But this night it wasn't for me to see. Not this night.

Nor the chevron of geese, heading for home, riding the wind, steering straight for the polestar. Only the night-shattering cry, haunting, calling, sending chills down my bones.

And so it passed on the moonless night at the beach. Prayers spilled like waves that I couldn't hear. Floating out to the heavens that seemed to be cloaked wholly in blackness.

Fitting, I thought, as I sat there unfurling each and every petition. I couldn't see God. Couldn't hear waves. Couldn't even make out the moon.

But in none of those instances did my lack of sensation suggest absence of any kind, nor mean that nothing was there.

Just because I couldn't hear flapping of wings, didn't mean the geese were not flying.

Just because I couldn't hear luffing of waves to the shore, didn't mean the lake had gone dry.

And so with the God whose moon was lost behind clouds.

It all surrounded me, every last bit of creation. And, yes, too, Creator.

Faith is the thing that comes to you when you kneel in the dark on the sand in the night. And the lone goose calls to you, tells you it's there, up above.

Holy Week

*A*ll week in this old house, we've been burrowing deep into ancient and timeless stories. The story of the Exodus, *Pesach*, the retelling of the Jews' escape from slavery in Egypt, a retelling that Elie Wiesel, the late great Nobel Laureate and Holocaust survivor, called "a cry against indifference, a cry for compassion." It is a retelling stitched with blessing, and question, and story.

Its leitmotif, "You were strangers in a strange land," God's words to Abram, a call to radical empathy, a call to ever open our hearts to those who are strangers, marginalized, in our midst.

After three nights of Seder, of coming to tables filled with people we love, after cups of wine, and reciting of plagues, after singing *Dayenu* (the Hebrew word for "enough," as in God's love would have been more than enough, in a rising series of praises; "If God had only created the world and not brought us out of Egypt, it would have been enough"), we pivot to the holiest hours of Holy Week—or I do anyway.

I am deep now and deepening. I hear the cry of my soul, being pulled into timelessness, into sacred hours and space. I burrow into the stories of the Last Supper (the Seder of Jesus and his twelve apostles), of Gethsemane, of the betrayal by Judas, of the mocking and crowning with thorns, of the bone-crushing cross shouldered by Jesus as he stumbled along the trail to his crucifixion at Golgotha, the hill just outside Jerusalem, the hill where he cried out, "Father, why have you forsaken me," and then, "Father, forgive them, for they know not what they are doing." The whole arc of anguish and redemption in two short utterances.

It never fails to draw me deep into the nautilus of prayer.

Good Friday

Daybreak

It is our humble conviction that the divine and the human meet in the slightest detail in the seamless garment of God's creation, in the last speck of dust of our planet.

—*Ecumenical Patriarch Bartholomew*
as quoted by Pope Francis

It's holy ground, the acres and acres that invite us in, to begin a close and careful examination. To witness the astonishments the earth offers up, offers forth.

And so, at the dawn of this Good Friday, this holy Friday, I walk in silence, and I whisper the prayer of the earth once again unfurling in beauty. Earth knows just how parched our soul might be in this the season of starting over again.

It's the garden, the woodland, the gurgling of the winter's thaw in the creek, these are the places that animate the coming back to life—of the earth, and the curled-up spirit within me. The one that just might find the courage to reach once again for the softness of springtime's return.

I take to heart the words of dear Pope Francis, quoting the Patriarch Bartholomew. I subscribe to the belief that God wrote the Book of Nature, and that each and every unfurling tendril, each and every bulb that shoots down roots and shoots up that periscope of green, each and every quivering of feather or leaf, it's all here to whisper the presence of the Divine and Holy Wisdom. All we need do is plunk ourselves amid its quiet narrative; all we need do is pay attention, and the lessons and learnings will tumble upon us. Breathe healing into our brokenness. Breathe hope into our hollows. Breathe, again and again, the story of resurrection, of life tiptoeing in to all the moments and places where we thought only death was left in the wake.

Afternoon's Silent Vigil

The sky is gray. As it should be. As my mama long ago told me it would be, had to be. This was the day that Jesus hung on the cross. This was the day they call Good Friday, though I never have understood that, never will understand that. It's a Friday when I will carve out a hollow of silence. I will wrap myself in silence and gray, gray sky.

It's my practice, because we don't usually shake off the ways of our earliest days, to contemplate deep and hard these hours when the one who healed the sick, threw out the tax collectors, the one who preached "Love your neighbor as yourself," who wept in the Garden of Gethsemane, he was stripped, and crowned with thorns. He carried the cross of his own dying along the dusty road to Golgotha. He fell down, three times. And then, when he came to the place where he was to die, his hands and feet were nailed to limbs of tree, to wooden timbers, and he slowly breathed his last. Before he dropped his head, he called out: "Father, forgive them, for they know not what they are doing."

I never get to the bottom of it. But every year, come this gray, gray Friday, I try. I sink deep into what might have been coursing through a holy man on his way to die. I contemplate how it might be to live a life of trying to right the ways of a world that's side-stepped what matters, that's lost sight of how to love, of what it means to make peace with enemies, to embrace the cast-aside, the forgotten, the scorned. And then, at the end of that short life, to be condemned to die. To carry the weight of that cross knowing it's the instrument of your own death.

All of that I contemplate in silence. It's one rule from long ago that I try mightily to abide by. My mama made us all be silent. Not a word from noon to three, the hours when Jesus hung on that cross, the hour when he died. Long ago, on all those gray, gray Fridays, I tiptoed to my bedroom, my one sanctuary in a house of four brothers. I sat on my bed, stared out the window at the sky, turned the pages of some evocative telling of those final hours. And waited for the sky to darken, maybe rumble, maybe cleave, at the stroke of three, the hour when Jesus died.

And so it is, here and now, the silence that will infuse the afternoon, when I will retreat to my room, stare out the window, turn the page of some evocative retelling of this gray, gray Friday. I will follow alone the rule of silence.

There is eloquence in silence, particularly amid this cacophonous world. There is wisdom in allowing thoughts to flow, to follow their course deep down to where the inklings come. Or the knowing. It's as if the rivulets of thawing spring find their way to rushing creek, where the bubbling up begins.

It's rare and it's a gift, this setting aside an afternoon for silence. For holy thought. For deepening.

And this gray, gray Friday, there is much to contemplate. To breathe deep and fill my soul.

Mothering Day

*H*ere we are on the brink of the day when, for one short whirl of the sun, we hold mothering up to the light. My prayer, this and every day, is that we catch a glimpse, a deep glimpse, of its glories. That we think deep and hard about the difference that motherlove has made in our lives, how it allowed us to catch the updraft, how it dried our tears and set us on our way. How it always, always listened. How maybe it whispered, every once in a while, "You are so beautiful, so brave, so blessed."

Your motherlove might not have come from your mother. But, surely, there was someone somewhere who loved as a mother loves. And you learned, perhaps, to love in that way.

It's a whisper to every motherer everywhere: you do magnificent work, holy work. What you do, day after day after day, long night after long night, year after year—it matters. Deeply. You do the work that stands the best hope of healing the wounds and the tatters of this tired old world. The balm—the attention, the love without end—it pours from your heart, if you let it, if you will it. And the world so desperately needs it.

Motherhood is not for the faint of heart, and the heart needs to triple in size, so it seems, to pack in the requisite vast and infinite wisdom—and patience and sheer calculation and imagination and stamina and worry and second-guessing and, yes, full-throttle pangs of remorse when we get it wrong, time after time.

And motherhood holds no escape clause. We're in it for keeps.

What other adventure known to humankind might find you taking a little child by the hand, just after a soggy afternoon's rain, and heading out the door in search of worms that might need rescue, plucked from the unforgiving concrete sidewalk and tenderly placed in the oozy garden? Or have you witnessing, from the very front row, the moment when mixed-up alphabet letters on a page suddenly rearrange themselves into equations called words, and the child is off and reading?

Oh, it takes love, all right. Deep-veined love. The sort that reroutes all the wires inside you. That literally re-scripts your dreams, gives

center stage to the newest, dearest soul in
your life, one you suddenly realize you can't
live without. And for the
first time ever, perhaps, you
know that you'd throw yourself,
in an instant, before a car or a train
or a boulder barreling toward that babe
who looks in your eyes as if his life depends
on you.

Because, truly, it does.

Well, there are rare few chances in this board game
called A Life in which to pull out all the stops, to give it
everything you've got, to score one more chance to do it right,
to love with all your heart.

Doesn't matter to me if the child comes by birth or by heart, or
simply wanders down the sidewalk and finds a place on my couch.
It's a nasty speed-chase out there, with cars flying into ditches right
and left. If the walls within which I dwell happen to offer rare respite,
time out, breathing room, a place where dreams can be launched
and hurts aired out to dry, well then I'm posting a shingle on my
doorpost: "Time out offered here."

I think often—expend a bumper crop of brain cells—on the subject of growing kids. It's religion to me, the holiest sort. It matters more than anything else I will ever do. Closest thing to curing cancer. Because it boils down to taking the heart and soul you've been handed, and tenderly, wisely filling both with light. Considering them stealth missiles of planetary illumination. The answers to a Peace Prize prayer.

There's not a creature on the globe who wouldn't pray to be loved deep and pure and forever after. It's the highest hope of all creation.

It just might be most every blessed mother's story: we stumble upon the best that we can be, sometimes, when living, breathing, squawking, ever-hungry babe is cradled in our arms. Our trembling arms, to be sure. Our arms that grow stronger, surer, over all the sagas and the chapters and the countless hours of two lives entwined.

I stand in wide-eyed wonder. I bow down low in deepest gratitude. I wince at my mistakes, moments I'd give anything to do over. And I marvel at the times when I stepped to the edge of the precipice, mustered all my courage, and leapt—that eternal lifesaving instinct nestled deep in every mother's heart, the one that propels us to put form to whatever is the holy vow we take when we're first told that life stirs within.

We hope, we dream, we pray. We reach down deep, deeper than we ever reached before. We listen until the birds of dawn begin to sing, if that's what it takes some long, dark, hollow nights.

We find our voice along the years. We exercise our heart. We rack our brain. We love, and love some more.

I'm struck, often, and saddened, at how dismissed mothering can sometimes be. In a world of power suits, apron strings were relegated to the back of the pantry. Even though every one of us knows how deep a blessing it is to be mothered by a full-throttle motherer, one who deftly knows when to hit the gas and when to let up—when to be the hand at the small of the back and when to stand quietly off in the wings (whispering wholehearted incantations the whole while)—I think we sometimes forget, as a society, the power and magnitude of mothering. We forget, perhaps, how deeply this world needs what we know, what we do, endlessly and tirelessly.

One last thing: I would like to make the day not plain old Mother's Day, a noun. Which by my take is exclusive, too exclusive.

I would like to add an *-ing*. And make it Mothering Day, beckoning the verb. A day for all who mother.

Not just those who know what it is to have pushed the burning bulge as if your life depended on it. And not just those who've signed their name on someone's dotted line. Or stepped in without official papers.

All of that is fine. Amazingly, awesomely, only-MotherGod-could-have-invented-this, so very fine.

But there is more—there *are* so, so many more.

Yes, every last someone who has stroked a brow, wiped a tear, dabbed chocolate off a little cheek, fluffed a pillow, tucked in the covers, whispered bedtime prayers, set an extra place at the table, stretched a meat loaf, picked the peas out of the pasta salad, kissed a bloody knee, kept a retching tot from falling in the toilet bowl.

Yes, every pair of arms that's lifted a dead-weight child in the pool, played red rover until the cows came over, pushed a kid on training wheels around and around the block, turned the pages of *Goodnight Moon* so many times you find yourself chanting goodnight to the mittens when no one's in the room.

You get the point.

May it be mothering, the art of tender caring, coaxing life, leaving mercy in your wake, the art that knows no gender bounds, no census-taker's definition, the art the world needs in mighty thronging masses, may it be mothering, and not just mothers, for which we stand and shout, "God bless you, each and every motherer."

The Infinite Wisdom of Springtime's— Or Any Season's—Waning

*A*nd here's the genius: just before we've had our fill, quite before we're fully sated, the seasons change, move on. The lily of the valley fades, and the peony rises. A part of us sags, aches for what we're losing, but then another beauty comes.

Like all of life and all its finest gifts, we're left wanting just a little more. One more sunset. One more snowflake. One more lazy afternoon. It keeps us ever on the verge. Ever alive to what's slipping away, what's on the rise. We're infused with pang of loss, and delight at the replenishment.

Truth is, all of life's ephemeral. Nothing lasts. Nor is forever. There is not a drop to be taken for granted. And therein lies its edge.

As all the mystics tell us, as all the holy know, the more deeply we relish every succulence, the more fervently we pay attention, rapt attention, the more fully—and blessedly—we live this one whirl we call Our Life.

The Springtime Kitchen

Certainly, it's the farmer's field—asparagus bed, in particular—that captures the vernal imagination, and mine. But in my growing-up days, spring meant Easter holiday, which meant a six-hour road trip, Chicago to Cincinnati, and my grandma's ivy-covered house on the hill. Once our old wood-paneled station wagon pulled to a stop at the bottom of the scary-steep driveway just outside the butter-bathed kitchen, we couldn't escape the wagon's confines quickly enough. We'd be in my grandma's ample arms, then slither past—swift as politely possible—headed straight to the tin of Easter cut-outs tucked belly to belly against the toaster. Springtime to me will forever play the soundtrack of lifting the lid on a menagerie of chicks and bunnies, ducklings and lambs, and golden-edged eggs, all nesting atop crinkly wax-paper beds.

Oma Lucille's Famous Rolled Cut-Out Cookies

There was always a tin on the yellow pre-Formica counter. She had a habit of cutting flowers, mostly roses, from the pages of slick magazines. Precision cut. Glued, taped, somehow attached to the lid of the tin. Gilding the lily, really, because what was inside, in waxy blankets, was the taste of walking into Grandma's, and the sweet-baked perfume that, still, takes me back to North Cliff Lane, the street where my German Oma lived for half a century. As I look closely at the recipe card, I see a note that says this came from the kitchen of Elizabeth G., my grandpa's sister, Aunt Lily, yet another sturdy German baker, this one a Fräulein. Spinster sister, Aunt Lily was. Ah, but she begat these, and they live on, ever they do . . .

Provenance: My Great-Aunt Lily, Elizabeth Glaser

Yield: Never enough

> 1 cup shortening
> ½ cup brown sugar
> ½ cup white sugar
> 1 egg
> 2 cups flour
> ¼ teaspoon baking soda
> ¼ teaspoon salt
> 2 tablespoons lemon juice
> 2 teaspoons grated lemon rind
> Raisins, pressed into service as various body parts

Cream shortening. Add sugar. Cream well, adding egg, flour, soda, salt, and, finally, lemon juice and rind.

Chill about 3 hours (or overnight).

Preheat oven to 350 degrees Fahrenheit.

Roll to ¼-inch thickness.

Deploy cookie cutters. (Baker's note: As the season demands, bunnies, chicks, ducklings, lambs, Easter eggs in spring; pumpkins, turkeys, Santa à la sleigh, as their occasions arise.)

Plunk raisin where needed—bunny's nose, chick's beak, or, in time, Mr. Turkey's eye.

Bake 10 to 12 minutes, or until golden-rimmed.

Let cool, then slide off cooling racks and settle on wax-paper nests.

Summertime

Season of Plenitude

Abundance, the zeitgeist of summer. Emphatically, it's slow time, take-it-gentle time. The season for lollygagging down back roads, for dozy afternoons in the shade of the willow, or paddling in circles round the edge of a pond. It's when heaven and earth offer undiluted gifts: high-dose sunshine, thunderstorms that shake the rafters (and your old bones, while they're at it), silver-knotted domes of night so speckled with starlight you wonder who flicked all the switches. By summer's zenith, the farmer's plot is bent under the weight of its generosities. Succulence, the season's song. Our mothering might take its cues from the very same octave: savor these days, every last drop, as ephemeral as the swallowtail riding the southerlies. Shimmering past my nose one instant, gone the next. Indulge is summer's instruction. Unfurl a picnic. Pluck a berry from the brambles. Catch a firefly. Behold its blinking wonder. And while you're at it, behold the blessing of unfettered childhood, frame upon frame. Consider it the treasure you bequeath to the ones you love beyond measure.

Summertime's Wonderlist

it's the season of . . .

firefly flicker: the original flash of wonder . . .

fledgling's first flight, lesson in resilience . . .

cricket chorus, that chirpity blanket tucking in the nighttime, "audible stillness" in the poetry of Nathaniel Hawthorne . . .

butterfly couplet shimmering across the lazy afternoon . . .

sweet corn, buttered, dripping down your chin . . .

ditto: the peach . . .

putting thumb to the hose: water therapy at its most meditative . . .

Perseid's meteoric chalk marks etched across the blackboard of midsummer's predawn sky . . .

scribble your own summertime wonders here . . .

A Count-Your-Blessings Calendar

Blessed Be Summertime, Season of Plenitude

SUMMER SOLSTICE: *Celebrate the longest day to bask in sunbeams. Play shadow games. Count your freckles. Scatter sunflower seeds to the wind. Watch them grow, turn their heads to sun as if to nod their thank-you. From sunup to sundown, frolic. Marvel at all that mighty sun can do for little us.*

MIDSUMMER'S DAY (JUNE 24): *Praised be the prodigal light that ever rises and sets. Hidden through the night, it returns, peeking over the straight-edged distance, every dawn. That we might absorb the faithfulness and come to know: the light will always come.*

BLESSING 3: *Some consider it religion to grow a garden. Like any act of faith, it sometimes shatters hearts. But, more often, takes your breath away.*

INDEPENDENCE DAY (JULY 4): *Awaiting nighttime's fireworks: Is it not the darnedest thing that, when sitting at the drawing board, God thought to make a bug with taillights? Call it firefly or lightning bug or blinking-bellied beetle. Mostly, it's a gentle nudge if you're out in darkness: Burst of light will come. Promise* blinking in the distance. Hope is here, the taillight tells you, even when you cannot see it. And then, the flash.

BLESSING 5: Make daily rounds of the growing things in the so-called garden. Carry clippers. Cut a new bouquet every day. Tuck them in odd places, like next to children's beds, just to see if anyone notices. Whisper vespers for the lovelies.

BLESSING 6: "But there is still one more thing I have to do," said Miss Rumphius, in the eponymous children's picture book by Barbara Cooney, a story worth committing to heart. "I have to do something to make the world more beautiful." And so she set out to scatter lupine seeds. "All that summer Miss Rumphius, her pockets full of seeds, wandered over fields and headlands, sowing lupines." What will you sow upon this holy Earth?

BLESSING 7: Praised be this season of high permeability, when the outside comes rushing in, in great gulping doses through wide-open windows. And the inside, too, stirs to life, especially in nighttime, in the dappled dark, with but a moon or flickering street lamp draping your bedclothes in filigree shadows.

BLESSING 8: Praised be, too, the summer's night sounds gurgling in. The 10:04 train whistling by. Horns and siren, reminding that all is not still. Perhaps you've a balcony seat on cat fights. Or worse, the spine-chilling warble of a nest of innocents being attacked. Primal and raw, it all comes in the night. Unfiltered. The world as it is.

NATIONAL BLUEBERRY MUFFIN DAY (JULY 11): Be rebellious: make blueberry pancakes instead. Lift a fork to so much joy jam-packed inside a tender globe of berry, nature's tiniest juice balloon. Beholding joy, prayer distilled.

BLESSING 10: The Sisyphean summer task: Hour upon hour yanking weeds from the garden, where pushing and shoving among roots is getting out of hand. And weeds could win Best of Show. The meditation: what a gift to weed from your life whatever gets in the way of reaching toward the heavens.

BLESSING 11: Ponder the wisdom of Celia Thaxter (1835–1894), New England poet and author of An Island Garden: "In this hour divinely fresh and still, the fair face of every flower salutes me with a silent joy. . . . All the cares, perplexities, and griefs of existence, all the burdens of life slip from my shoulders and leave me with the heart of a little child that asks nothing beyond the present moment of innocent bliss."

BLESSING 12: There's no substitute for a summer's rain. No rinse of all the earth that so revives what dwells here. Summer's rain is balm, soothes parts of us we didn't even know were hurting. Till we hear the whoosh, or pit-a-pat. And then the healing washes over us.

BLESSING 13: Summer shower's postlude: the rainbow. Boils down to basics, pure and simple: light + water (in the form of rain or, in a pinch, straight from the hose) = arc of infinite color. That we might always see through to every moment's miracle.

BLESSING 14: Night prayer: Listening for rain in dry season, hear the rumblings of far-off thunder, like growling from the woods. Through the half-slept night, it's not unlike keeping one ear perked for a fevered child down the hall. We don't doze so soundly when we worry about the blessed things whose watch we keep. And we keep watch on parched and thirsty earth. When infusion comes, we bow down in deepest gratitude.

Summer's Sacred Instruction

*I*t comes without notice, like butterfly wings that waft before your face, your cheeks, the bump that ends your nose. You catch the barest shift of breeze, a quivering of light, you look up, you realize: something sacred just passed by. It came from who knows where, but along the way, it surely graced me.

And so it is with summer, with those wisps and darts of weightless wing. With the moments when the heaviness of all year long is suspended, when breeze blows through the screen, garden leaves flutter, light practically sparkles, and you feel your shoulders drop their heavy load.

Where summer settles best is in the soul. In the part of you that remembers not to worry for the moment. To soothe the long, ragged edges. To breathe.

School's Out: A Prayer for Beginnings and Endings

(Written at the close of the school year in which my firstborn, home after college, taught literacy at a tough inner-city school, humbled every day by struggling-to-read kindergarteners through eighth-graders. Written for both my boys—one teaching, the other still being taught—and all who've come to the end of another school year. Just as emphatically, this prayer is a nod to the practice of pausing amid the rhythms of life, ticking through our litanies of gratitude as one chapter closes and another begins . . .)

*F*irst and always, thank you, dear God, for keeping them—all of them—safe. Specifically, for each and every drive back and forth on streets where guns aren't foreign, aren't far away, where jersey barriers and plain-clothes cops (guns drawn) have been known to block the route. Thank you for steering that bullet clear of anyone's flesh the day it shattered the schoolroom window, bounced off a pipe, and dropped to the hard tile floor of the preschool classroom. And thank you, while I'm at it, for inspiring my firstborn to stick it out till the end of the year, and not abandon the classroom. Not even on the days when one second-grader pushed another clear down the stairs, or the pair of sixth-graders devised the science experiment, the one where they shoved their pinkie fingers straight into the electric socket to see what would happen. And not on the day the fourth-grader called him a name you wouldn't want a kid to know. And not on the day when the fifth-grader punched him—hard—in the gut.

Thank you for the hours when you gave them strength, all of them, no matter the obstacle, or tight-walled passage. The days when the soccer coach picked the other kid, the day when the test they'd hoped to ace came back not even close. The day when the job that somebody wanted was already filled.

Thank you for the wisps of kindness that softened their days. Thank you for the rare few times when I might have unearthed just the right thing to say. When I answered the phone, drove to the schoolhouse door without grumbling, and knew once in a while that the holiest sound I could make was the silence of listening, just listening.

Thank you, too, for the joys. For the love birthed in someone's heart, and the delight of watching him tenderly bake her a batch of congratulations cookies. And ice them, to boot. Each one inscribed with a word or a phrase that signaled their shared secret script.

Thank you for the undeniable fact that they surround themselves with very fine friends. Friends there in a pinch. Friends whom the little one says "make me a better person." And friends who thought nothing of flying in for the weekend, halfway across the country, simply because it's the place my other kid calls home (or at least this year he does).

Thank you for the dinners that left the kitchen looking like a battalion rolled through. And thank you for the quiet dinners for four, especially the ones when no one minded the leftovers. Thank you—yes, thank you—for the chance to pack two lunches again. And thank you, mightily, that the last one of the year has been packed. The PB&J, retired for the summer. Or at least *my* spreading knife.

Thank you for all of this, always. Thank you for the blessing of pause. Of paying attention to cusps, of beginnings and ends. Thank you more than anything for this latest whirl around your radiant sun. I know I'm sated. I'm shining.

Meditations for Summer

*F*or me, *summering* is a verb with pages to turn. It's sipping slowly from tall, sweaty vessels of lemony water. It's slapping away mosquitoes, and keeping watch for the firefly. It's taking time out and not feeling guilty. It's feeling like Friday afternoon stretches for days. It's relishing: a balsa wood baskets of berries; fat spears of asparagus charred from the grill; a book I don't want to end; daybreak with a hot mug of coffee; mama wren enchanting with her motherly duties; nightfall with a flute of prosecco.

It's the one time of year that begs us to savor the succulence. To consider the high art of nonchalance and lull without purpose. It's the deep-down knowing that if you're turning a page, staring into the distance, or keeping watch on a wren, you are more than doing your job. You're inhaling the whole of the blessing, the one that now is upon us: welcome to summer.

We were slowing time. We were holding up the hours, sinking deep into the pure and simple gift of being side by side.

Love is like that. Love needs little embellishment. Time—hours upon hours stacked together, in one fell swoop—that's plenty. That's priceless.

There is nothing so fine as falling asleep in a house where every bed is filled. Where the sounds of doors closing, sheets being thrown off, odd faucets shushing in unfamiliar rhythms, is lullaby to sleep.

And so, you hold time, you hold all that fills these hours, as fully and preciously as you know how. You glide through a day savoring. Sinking wholly into what's before you, all around you. You know that soon the distance once again will come. The miles and miles between you. The necessity of phone line. The certainty that law school and life will make these sorts of days just that much more out of reach.

I might call it the fireworks rule. Do something kind, do something crazily wild, driven by love, and don't tell a soul that you've done it, then wait for that tickle, that pop, that night sky of sparkle and light, rising up from deep down inside. It's the lightning bolt of adrenaline, perhaps, oxytocin oozing all over. It's God, maybe, tapping you there on the heart, whispering, "Hey, sweetheart, high five. That's what I'm talking about when I talk about love. Love and love madly. Love with abandon."

Are we not working to learn to cup in our hands the holiest waters of life as they're poured? Might we not look to the monarch butterfly, who alights on the milkweed amid his long flight, who settles and sips, who quells for a moment his orange-speckled flittering? Aren't we, too, trying to stop, take a drink, quench the unquenchable thirst?

A Quartet of Ponderings for a Slow Summer's Day

My whole life long one of my hungriest appetites has been for words. To this day, I toss back handfuls of words the way some might do with Milk Duds. I can suck on a single word the whole day long: unspool, lollop, stippled, susurration, *pick one, any one; each a concoction of syllables as delectable to me as a lemon sour might be to you. When I stumble upon a particularly delicious snippet of wonder, wisdom, or plain old esoterica, I hoard it away in the pages of my all-purpose lexical repository, the commonplace book. Here, a handful of delectables I might savor all in a summer's day.*

*B*e audacious is the point. Love audaciously, the insistence.

"Don't think that every gift of grace, every act of kindness, isn't a quake that moves another heart to give, that grows into an avalanche of grace," writes Ann Voskamp in her achingly beautiful book, *The Broken Way: A Daring Path into the Abundant Life.* "What if the truth really is that every tremor of kindness here erupts in a miracle elsewhere in the world?"[1]

May we all quiver with kindness, every blessed day. And may miracles erupt here, there, and everywhere.

The Zen Buddhists teach us well, and Muslims too: Take time out of your day. Carve deep places for quiet contemplation. And don't forget the prayer of the unplanned picnic.

Consider this morsel from "Drifting," a poem by Mary Oliver, who is something of a patron saint of poetry for me, especially because she bequeaths us lines that, in the plainest speak, illuminate shimmering sacred truths. Here, amid a walk in the rain, her thoughts drift, unwittingly, to God. She startles, drawing this fine and profound distinction: "How God, or the gods, are invisible, / quite understandable. / But holiness is visible, entirely."[2]

That we might always see—be astonished by—holiness, entirely.

Lastly, this: In her breathtaking "Little Summer Poem Touching the Subject of Faith," our prophet of paying attention,

Mary Oliver, writes how every summer she listens and looks "under the sun's brass and even into the moonlight," but can't seem to catch summer in its act. She can't hear anything, can't see anything, "not the pale roots digging down, nor the green stalks muscling up, nor the leaves deepening their damp pleats." Yet day upon day, the summer fields grow taller, thicker, lusher. Confessionally, she claims to fail as a witness, seeing nothing, deaf to the faintest of ticks, the tapping down of the roots—all of it happening "beyond seeable proof, or hearable hum." But her lament pivots to imploring, in words that might echo our own deepest prayer: "[T]herefore, let the immeasurable come. / Let the unknowable touch the buckle of my spine."[3]

She immerses us in our wrenching inadequacy to wrap our hands around the ineffable. And then, in a single sweep, she reconciles us to the ecstasy that lies in the touch of its breath. "Little Summer Poem" is a beauty, worth reading in whole. Worth committing to heart. And, surely, to soul.

Summer's Blessed Balms

The Holy Balm of the Garden

I couldn't break the spell. The spell of taking time to sink my toes into the deliciousness of a summer's day. A hot and sweaty day. Or a cool and cloudy day. Didn't matter. It was only in the act of whole-body immersion, of flinging my old self into the elements—thorns that scratch, dirt that worms its way under fingernails and toenails, sun that beckons freckles to come out of hiding—that I was able to find a way to untangle the brokenness of my heart, to put a breath of pure, soft air back into my lungs.

Of course I know—full well—that it's all just distraction. But somehow, deep in the ministrations of gardener to garden, of human hands to tender growing things, I found a way to exercise an urge to heal, to fix, to chase away the hurt, the ugliness, that had descended on the planet: yet another siege of senseless killings. Day after day, hour upon hour, there comes darkness in forms we can't imagine. And so we're left with the scant few things we know, to bring back light. To sow seeds of tenderness and love. Of holiness, perhaps.

To lose a day, or a week, upside down or sideways in the garden, is to find a thread that just might stitch us close to whole again. Or at least steady us enough to tumble forward. Till the next bee buzzes along. And once again we're swept away by wonder, antidote to that which leaves us broken.

Balm of the Motherly (and Fatherly) Sort

Sometimes even parents play pretend. Because they have to. Because sitting there falling apart would not help. Would not do a thing. So we pretend that we've all sorts of lotions and potions and balms. We dab cream on a cut, make it feel better. Whip up concoctions to take out the sting. We do voodoo and rain dances, for crying out loud. Whatever it takes to get over the bumps.

Balm for a Heart Broken by Baseball

In the wake of a rather, um, lopsided Little League game that ended, according to a little slugger's count, in a loss of 45 to 2, and not a few tears. It was the first game of the season, the first, but certainly not the last, of life's crushing defeats. Lessons learned on the sandlot extend far beyond how to lob or swing or slide into home. And the first-aid kit demands far more than mere Band-Aids.

Sure thing, I'll need to find a way to dust him off or, better yet, point him toward some saving grace, some truth, to steady him, to remind him, after all, it's not the final score that shows you who the winner is.

Be Safe: The Heart of Motherprayer

*A*nd that's when I realized, once again, that motherprayer is so much more than words. It's what we do and breathe.

It's stirring oatmeal before the crack of dawn, it's using half a roll of tape to seal shut, to protect, a box of sundries for a college dorm room, as if in simple acts of stirring, sealing, we can wrap our children—even when they're no longer little ones—in a sacred shield of holy light.

Impenetrable, we pray. "Be safe," the final words we whisper every time. Words that, now, mean so much more than simply, "I love you." That's understood, implicit.

"Be safe" is poetry, is vessel, for "I would die if you were hurt, were harmed."

"Be safe" is hope and faith boiled down into two short syllables. "Be safe" is the last line of defense, the thin membrane on the other side of which prayer and holy angels pick up the load.

Be safe, the holy mantra of the mamas . . .

Be safe. What more is there? What deeper prayer does a mother's heart hold? Above all, be safe.

Prayer for a Camper

*D*ear Mother God of woods and tangled roots, of see-through lakes, and dawn's first light, of moonbeams drooling on the meadow grass, and birdsong waking up the day,

I have delivered to you my precious child, my tender heart, brave heart. He is yours now, for two whole weeks, yours to hold, to guide along the trails in deepest, darkest night, yours to wrap your arms around in those shaky moments just before sleep comes, when thoughts drift home, when home feels faraway and hollow fills the void.

He is yours now as he leaps off the dock into soft-bottomed, sandy swimming hole. He is yours as he climbs the ropes and buckles onto that shiver-me-timbers woodsy trick, the zip line. He is yours as he climbs endless dunes and jumps for dear life. Hold those ankles straight, dear Mother Watcher God. Keep those bones from cracking into twos. Keep bees away, and while you're at it, please shoosh the darn mosquitoes. Ditto poison ivy.

Perhaps, too, you could drift down into the dingy cabin—he's in No. 6, in case that helps—and tap him lightly on the shoulder, whisper in his ear: "Don't forget the sunscreen. Slather on the OFF!" And when he loses things, say, the water bottle, or the flashlight, maybe just maybe you could guide his searching little hand to the very secret spot where said essentials are playing hide-and-seek.

Dear Mother God of star-lit dome, of lake breeze, of rustling in the cottonwoods, you now tend my first-time camper, you hold him to your moss-carpeted bosom. I pray you open up the woods to him, reveal to him the mysteries of your quiet ways, and your crashing-booming majesty.

For two short weeks, we've unplugged him just for you. He's all yours now. He has drawn in a deep, cleansing breath, shaken off his deep-woods worries, and surrendered to all the glories you have to offer him.

Tap his tender heart. Unspool for him the depth of confidence that's buried where he doesn't always know it dwells. Allow him to emerge from these woods, from these weeks along that crystal lake, from romping with the troupes of boys and abiding by generations-old rules of woodsmen's games, knowing just a bit more solidly how much he brings to this blessed world.

If so inclined, please be there when the hour comes, at last, for him to light his torch and lift it high—to illuminate not merely his way, but, as well, the twisting paths of all of those who walk beside him.

Hold him tight, dear Mother God, when he needs a squeeze, and be the wind beneath his wings when he glances down and sees that he is soaring, gliding where the eagles glide.

That's pretty much the whole of it from here on the home front, where I've nothing left to do but turn to you and trust with all my heart.

Thank you, Mama God, God of dappled afternoon light, God of pit-a-pat of summer rain, God who wraps the campers in her arms, and holds them safe and blessed ever after.

Rites and Vespers for the Season's End, Most Especially the Seasons of Mothering

I made a room that's something of a relic of the boyhoods I so loved. The ones where books were tucked in corners, slid from shelves, pages turned. The boyhoods populated by wooden blocks and trains. Now, a little chair sits empty. The alphabet rug, the one I once bought for a nursery, it's off at the cleaners and the rug repair shop. I seem to be preserving a chapter of our lives, pressing it onto the pages of my heart. A little part of me, perhaps, is hoping that some day a new crop of little people will climb the stairs, turn the corner and see the wall of books, and the bins of blocks and puppets. But mostly, I think, I'm making a room for me, the mama who will never ever forget.

A room where, when I walk in, I hear the echoes of boys from long and not so long ago. Where I pull any book off the shelf and turn a page, and suddenly I can picture the little hands and the voices who once begged for me to read that page over and over. And over.

The rooms in a house are like that, when they're no longer used. One by one, most houses surrender rooms to time. A room once strewn wall-to-wall with elaborate block constructions becomes a room with sweaty socks and inside-out jerseys. Years go by when you hardly see the floor. And then, there comes a dawn when the first beams of sunlight fall across hardwood slats that all but glow, so exposed they are, and not a hand puppet nor a book is out of place. When what you find in the morning is exactly as you left it at noon the day before.

But rooms hold memory, hold the rhythm of a heart that will not fade.

As certainly as the wooden soldier stands guard on the window ledge, as welcoming as the old bear now slumped against the wall, that room will harbor me. Will wrap me in its particular embrace. Will be my tucked-away respite at the top of the stairs.

For the days when I need retreat. For the days when all I want is to step back in time, to remember how it was and how we got here. For the days when nothing soothes my soul so much as the far-off whisperings of the room that grew my sweet, sweet boys. The room that holds my heart.

We come to deeper understandings of where we are in time, by circling all around our lives and the lives of the ones we love, to measure and mark just how we got here. It is as if in sifting, resifting, I am holding up each blessed frame of the time we have had so far. I am holding it up to the light. I am marveling. I am soaking one last drop. I am savoring.

Nearly eighteen years I have loved him more than anything, have been a player in the story of his life. Have known the scenes, most every one. And now, the ones I enter into, I hold on to in my mind, in my heart, as I commit to memory, yes, but even more to soul, the whole of this chapter of mothering. Of being the moon to his orbit, his everyday rotation.

I am gathering the frames, the moments of his wholeness, one facet at a time. I am doing what we do when someone we love is leaving, and we are making room inside our hearts to store the memories, the sense, the wholeness. I am holding on to time as I feel it slipping through my fingers. I am scaffolding my heart for when it's aching and these days are no longer . . .

One of the first things I learned when my kid went off to college—a steep climb of a first semester for me, not so for him—was that more than anything we'd stepped into the landscape of prayer.

The Summertime Kitchen

No-cook summer, the aim. Pluck tomato from the vine. Shake with salt. Consume. Repeat with the sweet pea, the runner bean, the cuke. And who ever met a berry that demanded more than a rinse—if that? Thus, the blueberry slump. A no-frills invention, concocted—lazily, one summer's afternoon—in the produce aisle. Even its verbs invoke indolence: dump, splash, dash . . . spoon and lick. With lick, though, comes a sudden surge of gusto.

Blueberry Slump

When indolence calls, per seasonal prescription. Once home from the market—farmer's or grocer's—bearing your bushels of berries (or simply a bulging pint), this charmer demands you reach no farther than the row of canisters, awaiting their mission. I happen to be besotted by the name alone— how could you not fall for a slump?—but you, like my boys, might succumb to the summery perfection of its mouth-popping indigo ooze.

Provenance: Once upon a summer's day, this receipt was unfurled by a friend I'd bumped into beside the berry bins; though long forgotten just who that was, the recipe charms on, vivid as ever.

Yield: I slump

> 2 pints blueberries
> 2 to 3 tablespoons fresh lemon juice
> cinnamon, a dash
> I cup flour
> I cup sugar
> I stick butter, cut into pea-sized bits

Dump the blueberries into a soufflé dish (Fear not, that's as close as we come to any sort of highfalutin *cuisine Française* around here.) Splash with 2 to 3 tablespoons fresh lemon juice and the cinnamon.

In another bowl, mix the flour, sugar, and butter.

(Baker's note: Add a shake of cinnamon to the baker's trinity above and, trick number 2, make it vanilla sugar, if you're so inspired. I usually am. All you need do to make your sugar redolent of vanilla bean is to tuck one bean into your sugar canister and forget about it. Whenever you scoop, you'll be dizzied by high-grade vanilla notes.)

Spoon, dump, pour flour-sugar-butter glop atop the berries.

Bake at 350 degrees Fahrenheit for half an hour.

(Oh, goodness, it bubbles up, the deepest berry midnight blue. Looks like you took a week to think it through and execute. Ha! Summer in a soufflé dish. *Sans soufflé.*)

Serve with vanilla ice cream. But of course.

Tiptoe out to where you can watch the stars, I was tempted to add. But then I quickly realized you might choose to gobble this up for breakfast, lunch, or a late summer afternoon's delight. In which case a dappled patch of shade will do.

Autumn

Season of Awe

O f all the seasons under the sun, it's amber-kindled autumn that most often brings us to our knees, leaves us jaw-dropped, heart wide open. As the earth turns toward longer, deeper star-bedazzled nights, and the dawn's first breath is brisk and brisker, we too begin our drawing in, drawing holy inspiration. So uncoils the nautilus of gratitude. Where better to begin the litany of thanks than at the edge of the farmer's field, where the harvest humbles us as the larder fills with bounty? Even that, though, pales as we move on to count the miracle of those we love. The Days of Awe, indeed, are upon us. The somber notes of autumn, scattershot with golden light, are certain calls to prayer. And our motherheart, the original expandable vessel, stretches deep and wide to hold whatever autumn brings, as the daily pace and its demands accelerate: high note, low note, radiance, or unrelenting shadow. We weather all.

Autumn's Wonderlist

it's the season of . . .

inflamed twilight sky, rosy-streaked, purple-bruised, ablaze with setting sun . . .

jolly pumpkins punctuating farmer's field . . .

the last aster, alone and proud, amid the shriveled diminishment of what had been the summer's shiningest hour . . .

the lonely cry of the unseen geese's night-crossing . . .

molasses light pooled across the windowsills, puddling onto hardwood planks . . .

pomegranate, impaled and gutted to reveal its belly's cache of garnet-seeded gems . . .

golden-glowing woods . . .

old quilts and thick bed covers, unearthed from their long summer's nap . . . .

scribble your own autumnal wonders here . . .

A Count-Your-Blessings Calendar

Blessed Be Autumn, Season of Awe

AUTUMNAL EQUINOX: *Blessed be the golden days and star-stitched nights of autumn. Blessed be triumphant blast of light, and jewel-toned tapestry, as the Northern Hemisphere lets out its final hallelujah before deepening, drawing in. And bless those among us who are wide-eyed to the wonderment.*

BLESSING 2: *Now's the interlude when leaves drop their drab, summer-worn green for jaw-dropping amber and gold, copper and crimson. Air turns wake-me-up chilly. The slant of sun drops in the sky, as we twirl farther and farther away, it is all autumn's call to attention.*

MICHAELMAS, FEAST OF ST. MICHAEL AND ALL ANGELS (SEPT. 29): *Considered "chief officer of Paradise," "vanquisher of evil," Archangel Michael slayed heaven's dragon in a great sword fight. As shooting stars streak across autumn's sky, we remember the sword's flash. And, as the dragon is said to have fallen into a blackberry bramble, we feast on the season's last blackberries while considering the evils we must vanquish from our lives.*

FEAST OF ST. FRANCIS OF ASSISI (OCT. 4): Contemplate the tenderness of the patron saint of woodland critters, who quelled swallows, tamed a wolf, befriended a cricket, and sang with nightingales. His early disciple, Thomas of Celano, marveled in the thirteenth century: "In everything is a scintilla of the goodness of God, and Francis, 'being completely absorbed in the love of God,' clearly perceived this goodness 'in all created things.'"

BLESSING 5: There is faith galore in tucking in a bulb, concentrated life. Setting it just so, roots poking down, shoot facing skyward, where vernal sun will one day tickle it awake, coax from frozen earth, startle us with tender slips of green. Resurrection, sealed beneath the earth.

BLESSING 6: Wrap yourself in the prayerful cry of the cello, the orchestra's autumnal offering. No deeper plea for hope than Bach's "Cello Suite No. 5 in C Minor." Might it be the backdrop to your autumn vespers?

BLESSING 7: Behold the piercing, minor-key dissonance, raining from on high. It's the trumpet blasts of geese in Vs. Amid this season of migration, as feathered flocks follow heaven's call, consider the words of John Milton, English poet and polemicist, who said of geese: They are "intelligent of seasons." Oh, that we all would be.

BLESSING 8: Some call this "the wabi-sabi season," so defined as the season that pulses with the beauty of sadness and the sadness of beauty, and the breathtaking poetry of imperfection and impermanence. Embrace your own wabi-sabi self.

ALL SAINTS' DAY (NOV. 1): A radical thought about saints: we each, all of us, possess sparks of the Divine. Our

*holiest charge: Kindle the light. Touch one flame to
another. Before it darkens. If we each spend one minute,
one spark of the day, living beyond
our small little selves, fairly soon
we've ignited a bonfire.*

*BLESSING 10: Bless the miracle of the monarch, the
one of all 24,000 species of butterflies who migrates the
farthest. For most of the year, the monarch lives an ephemeral
life. Within weeks, it dies. Not so autumn's monarchs, the
Methuselah generation—named for the Bible's oldest old
man, who lived "969 years" (Gen 5:27). Monarchs born
at summer's end live eight months. They exist for one purpose:
to fly south, and, come spring, beget the next generation. Who in heaven's
name dreamed up such almighty wonder?*

*BLESSING 11: Treat yourself to midnight's moon lace. Tiptoe to a
window—or straight under heaven's dome. When the moon is nearly full, behold the
moonbeams as they spill. All the earth, in dappled shadow. Better than Chantilly,
sure to take your breath away.*

*BLESSING 12: Regard the autumn frost: Miracle of sunbeams captured in wee globes
of dew, flash-frozen. Or might it be the cold sweat of dawn's labor, the hard work of
night turning to day? Either way, let it take your breath away. First blessing of the day.*

*THANKSGIVING: "Contemplation is life itself, fully awake, fully active, fully
aware that it is alive. It is spiritual wonder. It is spontaneous awe at the sacredness
of life, of being. It is gratitude for life."—Thomas Merton, Trappist monk, mystic,
writer (1915–1968).*

BLESSING 14: As you begin kindling wicks, come nightfall, consider the honeybees' hard labor to beget the beeswax. It's estimated bees fly 150,000 miles to yield one pound of beeswax. As Bavarian thinker Karl von Leoprechting wrote, in 1855: "The bee is the only creature which has come to us unchanged from paradise, therefore she gathers the wax for sacred services." Ponder that when next you illuminate the darkness.

Rapt: An Autumnal Blessing of Gratitude

We're easing into the deep of it. Or perhaps it's that the deep is deepening and we're being immersed. Being wrapped in it. Rapt.

Rapt would be my posture of late.

rapt /rapt/ *adj.* 1. completely fascinated and absorbed. 2. *literary* filled with intense and pleasant emotion.

Oh, I am rapt.

By night, the windows are open, and the hum doesn't come from air conditioners down the block anymore. They've gone quiet—at last. Now, the night belongs to the low-simmering song of the cricket, and the rising chorus of dawn. And the breeze. Curtains quiver. Bedsheets do too. Rather than flinging them off, I'm just as apt to pull them taut around my shoulders, up to my chin. And the moon. Did you happen to drink that one in? The harvest moon on the rise last night, the one that ignited the blue-black, silver-stitched dome, the one that cast moon shadow every which way. The one that promises even more when it rises tonight, in its fullest wholeness. . . .

These are the days when to be alive is to be rapt in prayer. I know I am. All day, hour upon hour, I feel the brushstroke of the Divine gentle against the nape of my neck, the small of my back, the bare flesh of my arms. And, surely, it's prayer that keeps my heart pulsing.

Every blessed act of each day—whole strings of the tiniest, mostly unnoticed (tucking a fresh vase of blooms by the side of my little one's bed, sliding an after-school snack onto the counter, knowing he'll see it, hoping he'll know it's a whispered "I love you" set out in apples and crackers and cheese)—each one is a prayer without words. Each one is my heart and my soul offering up the closest I know to turning my hours over to God. To saying thank you for the breath and the heartbeat. Thank you for the chance to brush up against the holiness that is this amber-drenched September day, this one latest chance to absorb, yes, to inhale, yes. But even more to put my enrapture to work, to say thank you in my own small acts of paying attention, in my own small acts of love and tender kindness.

Because all around me is God's immeasurable magnificence, a tapestry of jeweled stitches that holds me rapt. So deeply, vigorously rapt.

Meditations on Burrowing into Books for the Soul

Vladimir Nabokov, the great Russian-born American novelist, critic, and lepidopterist, instructs us in how to read: "A wise reader reads the book of genius not with his heart, not so much with his brain, but with his spine. It is there that occurs the telltale tingle."

Rebecca Solnit, author of countless brilliant prose passages, instructs us in how to write: "Listen to what makes your hair stand on end, your heart melt, and your eyes go wide, what stops you in your tracks and makes you want to live, wherever it comes from, and hope that your writing can do all those things for other people."

I hum the loudest when I find myself tumbling into text, when whole chunks of an hour go by, and I am as busy with my scribbling as I am with my inhaling of words, of ideas, of penetrating thoughts.

My job, one of them anyway, is to read books for the soul. I still can't quite believe that counts as work, and that—rather than collecting garbage cans, or chopping carrots for vats of soup—I've somehow found my way to reading for work. Reading soulful books for work.

By my definition the soul is a broad-canvased endeavor. The soul is without boundaries, stretching from star-basted night sky to the meadow where Queen Anne's lace nods in the breath of morning's breeze. By my definition the soul is that thing that catches the beauties, the depths, the light and the shadow of life and life beyond our feeble capacities.

In my book, the soul—that thing that I'm reading to stir—is the catch basin of all that is sacred, of all that is dispatched from God. It's our job, us little people with our creaky knees and our hair that won't do the right thing, it's our job—or so I believe—to rumble through life on full alert, on the lookout for those barely perceptible moments when the shimmer of light on a leaf, or the way the dawn ignites the horizon, signal to us that God is near. No, God is *here*.

And if we listen, say, put our ear to the wind, or to the chest of someone we love, or if we simply sit quietly and all alone, we might hear the still small voice that whispers of love, of courage, of bold and emphatic action, of whatever is the holiest thing you needed to hear.

Because God does that. God wants us to

114

bump up against wonder. God wants us to feel the walls of our heart stretched and stretching. God wants us to rustle under the newness of a thought, or an inkling, that's never struck us before. Or the God I love does, anyway.

And so I go, as instructed, to read, to try to write, to capture those fleeting sparks of the divine, to catch them with my soul, and clutch them dearly to my heart.

Beginner Prayer

On the very first full day of first grade, a boy I love was stricken with a whopping case of butterflies at the thought of boarding a school bus, tucking books in a locker, sitting in a desk, and eating lunch far, far from the old kitchen table he'd known all his days. As darkness fell on the eve of that day, when sleep refused to come, I dug up a pair of red button hearts, one for his pocket, another for mine. I explained that he could give it a squeeze whenever he missed me, and I'd do the same, all through the day. In that way that six-year-olds so magnificently do, he wholly trusted that indeed this would keep us connected—by heart. It got me to thinking:

Isn't this a paradigm—a starter kit, a seed pot—for prayer? Isn't this how a child begins to grasp the mystery? How—wordlessly or otherwise—you can reach beyond your frangible self at any hour? How you might not hear a whisper in reply, might not feel the hand of God squeeze tight your fingers or softly lay a palm at the small of your back, but you might soon come to understand that God, tender God, is always on patrol, keeping watch, breathing hallowed susurrations to your unsettled soul?

A Page or Three from My Hebrew Prayer Book

On Shabbat, God's Holy Pause

The pause of Shabbat is God's command to put down toil, lift up holiness. Marvel at the simple gifts of consecrated quiet. It is God's promise, too, to fill the holy chalice that is us, leave us thirsting for not a single blessed drop.

It's the blessing of the Friday night dinner, a blessing like no other I have ever deep-breathed. As the week lurches to a close, as deadlines are met, and hustle and bustle hit pause, I circle in on final preparations. Candles stand erect on the table. Lids topple off the coterie of pots and pans. I blanket the challah—the loaf of braided egg bread that's a staple of Shabbat—with the cloth my firstborn penned with brightly colored markers long ago in kindergarten Sunday school. Wine will be poured.

And one by one, they'll trickle in, the boys I love. They'll have put their busy weeks, their worries and distractions, behind them. I'll strike the match, put flame to wick, and unfurl the first of the three blessings. Blessings for the sanctuary of time we've constructed Friday after Friday, just before sundown, according to ancient text and modern-day awe. For all time is holy, but on Friday nights when the table's set, the candles are burning, and the faces you love are the ones you look up to see, that's when the cloak of holiness drapes most certainly around your shoulders.

Tonight, we'll raise a glass of deep red wine, and my husband will lead us in the prayer we call "Grandpa's prayer," the *Shehecheyanu*, the blessing reserved for the most extraordinary times, the most sacred times. The times when you reach deep down to the bottom of your soul and pull up grace and blessing. When every pore of your being shimmers with the knowing of how richly, finely, you've been blessed, anointed by purest holiness.

And because I stumbled on my own Jewish prayer of blessing, of remembering, I too will recite words that stir me to full attention, words that make me bristle with deepest knowing of just how sweet the hour is, every blessed hour, and the turning of each season. And the knowing, too, that the ones we love are ever woven into the whole of who we are.

The prayer begins:

> In the rising of the sun and in
> its going down, we remember
> them.
> In the blowing of the wind and
> in the chill of winter, we remember
> them.
> In the opening of buds and in the rebirth of
> spring, we remember them.
> In the blueness of the sky and in the warmth of
> summer, we remember them.
> In the rustling of leaves and in the beauty of
> autumn, we remember them.
> In the beginning of the year and when it ends, we
> remember them.[1]

On and on, the litany cascades—a kaleidoscope of grief but even more a call to the truth that love never dies. When we're weary, or lost and sick at heart, when we have joys we yearn to share. Every hour, every turning of the season, we remember and remember. The prayer, the litany of remembrance, draws to this all-enveloping coda: "So long as we live, they too shall live, for they are now a part of us, as we remember them."

On the Days of Awe

The lamb has been ordered. The prayer books, slipped from the shelf. Soon, I will slice the pomegranate and begin to count the seeds. Are there really precisely 613, the same as the number of *mitzvot*, or commandments, as the sages taught, as I was told in whispers in a Kosher kitchen once upon a time?

I have been curious, asking questions, burrowing into the holiness of the New Year, the Jewish New Year, Rosh Hashanah, ever since I stumbled on that fine bespectacled fellow in the newsroom so long ago, decades ago now. And because I come to this beginning— this pause to behold the wonder of creation, original creation— with inquisitive heart, because question upon question tumbles before me, because one leads to another and another, I can't help but be drawn deep into what these days offer: these days offer awe.

They are called, quite precisely, the Days of Awe.

Awe, my dictionary tells me, is "a feeling of reverential respect mixed with fear or wonder."

Awe, my etymologists tell me, has deep roots in fear, and traces back to circa 1300, *aue,* "fear, terror, great reverence." The current sense of "dread mixed with admiration or veneration" is due to biblical use with reference to the Supreme Being. *To stand in awe* (early fifteenth century) originally was simply *to stand awe. Awe-inspiring* is recorded from 1814.

In my own dwelling inside these Days of Awe, I don't think too much about fear. I tend toward wonder. The God I know and sidle next to is not one who makes me tremble. Truth is, I'm most myself when I draw deep into the hollows of God. When I feel myself wrapped in the arms of the one who gave me breath, and question, and proclivities for awe.

Because this pause for holiness is at once still new to me and now familiar, because in many ways it's always felt as if I'd been waiting for reason to hold up these days, to hold up these autumn's-coming hours, I walk through them with all pores open. I love the pungent notes that will rise up from the pot on the stove, the one where lamb simmers alongside onion and celery and garlic, before the apples and raisins and cinnamon settle in. I love the way the molasses morning light pours across the page. I love each sentence I find on the page, especially the ones that startle me, give me pause, give me much to think about during the long hours in synagogue, during the long walks that will punctuate the pause, the anointing that makes the Days of Awe unlike ordinary time.

Because I am always, always drawn to the sage of all sages, Abraham Joshua Heschel, I pulled him, too, from the shelf this morning. I've been filling the shelves with Heschel for a long, long time. Even before I knew I'd be the one to share my husband's bookshelves.

This morning I found this from Rabbi Heschel, along with the pages of prayer that we will tuck under our arms and carry to the pews where the prayers will rise. Because it speaks to all of us who are inclined to turn in, to refuel in the depths of quietude, I share these fine Heschel thoughts as something of a blessing for these days when we pause for awe.

Here, from "On Prayer," found in the collection, *Moral Grandeur and Spiritual Audacity: Essays*, by Abraham Joshua Heschel:

Prayer is not a stratagem for occasional use, a refuge to resort to now and then. It is rather like an established residence for the innermost self. All things have a home: the bird has a nest, the fox has a hole, the bee has a hive. A soul without prayer is a soul without a home. Weary, sobbing, the soul, after roaming through a world festered with aimlessness, falsehoods, and absurdities, seeks a moment in which to gather up its scattered life, in which to divest itself of enforced pretensions and camouflage, in which to simplify complexities, in which to call for help without being a coward. Such a home is prayer. Continuity, permanence, intimacy, authenticity, earnestness are its attributes. For the soul, home is where prayer is.[2]

May you find your way home in this sacred span of time, the one that unfolds across the coming hours, the ones I've come to know and love as the holy Days of Awe, when I bow my head, my heart, my soul, and pulse with the wonder of creation, and my one small moment to revel in all its glories.

On the Day of Atonement

On the eve of Yom Kippur, the Day of Atonement, back when my little fellow was a fourth-grader, he discovered that he'd left at school the list of words for the weekly spelling test. It was eight o'clock, the night before the inquiry. So we'd driven back to school, banged on the doors, hoping to somehow get to the desk that held the list. No such luck. Back home, I sat down to send a note to the teacher, and instructed the little guy to cobble as many words as he could remember onto a list. Instead, he slid under the door a piece of paper with these words, "I am soooooo sorry I'll make you brekfast and coffe love Ted".

And he taught me everything I needed to know, about the heart of the Day of Atonement . . .

"I am soooooo sorry I'll make you brekfast and coffe love Ted"

All because of some runaway spelling words...

The child had grasped, without pausing for punctuation, without worry for vowels in absentia, the heart and the soul of atonement, of Yom Kippur, really, that somber string of breast-beating moments that is launched, according to the Hebrew calendar that is ours as much as the Gregorian keeper of days, at sundown tonight.

It is all about actively mending the brokenness. Not just whispers of hollow apology, but picking up thread and stitching sanctified wholeness. Weave and reweave.

Just yesterday I was talking to a wise and wonderful rabbi. We were talking about *teshuva*, the Jewish principle of repentance—repent and repair—the centerpiece of these Days of Awe, of the Day of Atonement.

"I have sinned, and for this I am heartily sorry."

The words of the Prayer of Contrition of my little-girl days.

Catholic or Jewish, Jewish or Catholic—is it not all a great swirl, a soup of humble I've-wronged-and-I'll-right-it?

We thought it was spelling words we were missing last night; in fact, we found deepest religion, a subject often best taught by the youngest and wisest among us.

The ones whose hearts are, still, tethered to heaven.

Instructions for Living from Ones Who Are Dying

*T*alk to anyone who's dying. Listen in on what the dying tell you matters most: curling up with a child—and a picture book—pressed against each other's curves. Sitting one minute longer on the edge of the bed while tucking someone in at night. Spooning one extra dollop of butter in the mound of mashed potatoes. Hearing the click of the front door that signals someone's home. Catching the moonlight dapple the bedclothes.

Have you ever heard how hard the dying pray for just one more round of gathering the tiniest glories of a day?

Not long after a dear friend of mine died, I found out that in her will she'd asked that I be the keeper of her "creative work," a mantle I accepted with heavy heart. Night after night, I sifted through her piles and piles of papers stashed in boxes. And then I picked up two stapled pages, curled and yellowed at the edges. It was a writing assignment from years before, following the prompt, "If I were to die in five minutes..." What followed was the most extraordinary enumeration of quotidian wonders, the things she would most miss—sleeping, the warm wood of an apartment floor, wet sand between toes, the sand going from warm to cool when the sun starts to set, kissing a man for the first time.

On and on, she plucked joy upon joy...

I wept knowing that when she wrote it, she never imagined her death would come so soon, too soon. The paper trembled in my hands.

I was struck, hard and deep, by the simplicity of the litany. The depth and dimension of each pulsing joy, now taken away.

She made me think hard about how our lives are stitched of thin but mighty threads, glimmering delicate threads, threads we'd be wise to notice, to run our fingers across, again and again, for they're what's woven into the beautiful whole.

Our lives, my friend now gone made me realize once again, are a textured tapestry of heartache and joy, of blessing and softness and shadow and light, of everyday wonders that awake us to the moment, so the moments slow to a pause, so we behold each blessed minute of our awareness, our awakeness, so each hour is relished for the gift that it is. So not an hour goes by unnoticed.

This is the second time in six months that I am saying goodbye to a blessed and beloved friend.

I know how both would answer the question: "Can we just have a day?"

The answer, the imperative, is this: seize the day. Seize it now. Make each hour holy. Do not allow the hour to fritter away, charred bits of time, lost to petty and insignificant slights.

Can we just have a day?

Can we just have a day to seal our hearts, to savor the joy, the truth, before it's tugged away from us? Can we revel in each other's laughter? Can we find the delight as we look out at the world passing by? Can we taste deliciousness, taste the whole of it? Can we dive deep into the well of each other's company, each other's undying love?

I can hear my friends now, both reaching up from their hours of shallow and shallower breathing, I can see the look in their eyes, the insistence, the impatience: seize the day, seize the hour or minute. Seize the time that is yours. And be guided only by love. Pure and simple.

Please, take this day. And make it holy, pure and simple.

In the rawest days following death, your head—your whole being, really—all but quivers with the newness, the wrongness, of this life that seems to have a hole torn in the thick of it. In the hours when the stories are churned, and told and retold, you pay keenest attention. You distill the essence, as if a potion that might just save you. You whisper the hardest truths of a life just lost, and you spin them into incantations, promises to the slipping-away friend that you'll never forget. You'll never, never forget to be alive in just the way their parting words implored.

"Keep marveling," wrote my friend who died in September, words she'd sent at the dawn of a summer's day when she was pulled to watch the sun rise over the lake, and wanted me, too, to never stop marveling. And then, in a text one week before she died, she wrote: "Xxx swirl love swirl love recipe for today" (she'd had no time for punctuation that morning, and I didn't need it).

Not many months before that very last text, exactly one year ago today, she wrote me an email that felt almost like haiku, or a Buddhist koan, wisdom refined to its purest: "blessings, blessings, more blessings. every minute is bonus. sun. birds. now."

My friend who died in March, she too left me with instructions. She wrote: "If you love the life you have, please, please, practice gratitude. Wake up every morning acknowledging just how much beauty is in your world. Pay attention to it, honor it and keep your heart and your eyes wide open. You won't regret it."

Here's the hard part: no matter how deeply you promise, no matter how fully you inhale the one sure thing you know—that the only way to be alive is to be infused with love—the certainties begin to fade. Or maybe they only get muddied. It's the stuff of being human that never fails to knock us at the knees.

We lose track of our promise to live each and every day as if it might be our last, and to ferret out all piddling nuisance and distraction. And it's not because we're fatalistic or showing off our Celtic obsession with the beyond that we make that promise in the first place, but only because it puts the sharpest edge to being alive.

Truth be told, it's these insignificant traps that clutch us by the ankles, that totter us from our vows to stick sure-footedly to a life lived beautifully, gently, blessedly. To stay above the fray, as if wafting with angel wings, hovering over the melee.

I try, with all my might, to resist the temptation. To not give in to the bitter impulse. To stay tuned to the wonder, the astonishment. It's being human that makes it so hard.

Which is why I walk around these days with two slips of paper in my pocket, slips I reach for as if prayer beads, whenever I need to fill my lungs—and my heart—with all that is holy, to discharge the everyday demons:

"swirl love swirl love recipe for today," reads one of those slips.

"Wake up every morning acknowledging just how much beauty is in your world," reads the other.

And so, on the days, in the hollows of hours, when my promises tumble from my heart, and I feel my knees begin to wobble, I reach my hand in my pocket, and I hold on tight to the last best instruction from my two beautiful friends now watching from heaven.[3]

A Few Things Worth Believing

On Believing in the Beautiful, and Daring to Let It Be Birthed

If you believe in the God of the Beautiful, if you believe that each and every one of us had the Beautiful breathed into us once upon our beginning, then it follows—there's no room, really, for arguing otherwise—that the Beautiful is rumbling around deep inside, just looking for the nearest exit, so it can be birthed, so it can come tumbling wholly and wildly or quietly and breathtakingly to life.

All we need some days is a hot blast of courage. And the willingness to live with the pins and needles that are certain to follow. Once we commit to birthing the Beautiful.

On Believing in Courage

I sometimes think of myself as a chicken. A wimp of the first order. I keep watch on folks who look to be brave, and wonder, "How, oh, how do they do that?" Here's a secret: sometimes when I talk to them, when we both unfold our hearts, I find out that they're just as scared as I am, but they shush away those nasty whispers. Or march headlong into them, never minding the awful bluster.

Of course, I have to remind myself—over and over and over— of that little truth. That the courage to face fears is sometimes simply plugging your ears to the noise, and deciding to hum your own little courage tune.

On Believing That Love Comes in Whispers

In my mother's book of life, the litany of love reads like this: clothes pulled from the dryer, folded, stacked, and delivered to your bedroom chair; hot dinner, complete with cooked frozen vegetables; houseplants given a weekly dose of fluids; children driven—without grumble—to where they need to be; soccer matches attended, even if they're in kingdom come at seven in the chilly morning.

She will quietly, wordlessly, go about the business of taking care of your house—or mine. Because to my mama it is in doing that we love.

My mother is not alone in stitching the tapestry of life with *petit point*, those fine-grained stitches not grand in scale, not at all, but the very threads that hold us all together, that make our lives just a notch more beautiful, more breathable.

Last night, a night when I had to be away, my mama didn't want my sweet boy coming home to an empty house at the end of his very long day. So she skipped what she'd planned to do—skipped hearing her only daughter read a few pages from her very first book at a charmed bookstore, one with paned windows and Oriental rugs and books bursting from the shelves. My mama went, instead, to my house, to turn the hall light on. To press her hand to the door handle when a tired fist knocked. She was there to warm up the orange chicken she'd made two nights before. To scoop out peas in butter sauce.

And there she sat, with the boy we all love—so he wouldn't be alone while his mama was off reading and his papa was far away gathering notes for a newspaper story.

My mama stayed home at my house last night because she knew—without words—that it was the purest form of love that she could ladle out for all of us, not least of all for me, always torn when pulled away from where I, too, know I most belong.

My mama, once again, taught us, with so few words, that there's no headline-grabbing heroism in a certain brand of loving. But in the end, the very end, those small acts of utter selfless majesty are the surest holy gospel we could ever know.

On the Holy Wisdom of the Child

I was the one who slid onto the sheets, curled in a ball, and lay there, eyes closed. Just breathing. Feeling the rise and fall of my chest. Hearing my heart. My heart that all day had felt as if it were trudging a mountain. Or cracking in half.

That's when the boy who struggles with words, the ones that get jammed in the lead of his pencil, climbed in beside me and spoke: "Are you hurt? Are you worried? Are you tired?"

"You need to sleep," he said, touching my hair.

"Grown-ups," he told me matter-of-factly, "are more important than kids. You want your grown-up to stay alive to keep you safe."

He started to put his hands to the back of my nightgown. He made little circles where the angel wings might have started to sprout, back when God was deciding if we'd be the species with wings or without.

He was the putter-to-bed, this long, achy night. It was my little one, with his hands and his words, who woke me from my overdrained stupor. I didn't move, didn't flinch, but I tell you my spine tingled.

Had I not wanted to scare him I would have sat suddenly up. His words pierced through to my heart.

I whispered them back, as if a refrain. "You want your grown-up to stay alive to keep you safe."

I realized that was his prayer. Mine too. *Dear God,* I whispered so no one could hear, *give me strength.* The sort of strength I'd needed before. The strength to get up a mountain. To look out from the summit.

I lay there absorbing the gospel according to the one whose head shared the pillow. I lay there thinking how God speaks to us, some hours, in the voice of a six-year-old boy.

I lay there feeling the tenderness, feeling the power of his wisdom. I marveled long and hard at the miracle of how the teacher speaks to the student at the hour of absolute need.

I marveled at the clairvoyance of a child. How a child sees through the thick of a heart, through the tangle. How a child, as if a surgeon who works with microsized scalpels, can incise right to the core of the matter. Can feed in the words that the heart needs to hear. Can wake up even the sleepy.

Grace

Grace is balm for the soul. It feeds us in places that growl with unworldly hunger. It moistens the parts that are parched. Grace is the prayer beads we string in a row. The rosary of life lived at attention. It's the layer of soul tied to Divine. And it comes unannounced most every time.

It comes, grace does, like the brush of the great palm of God, there on your brow.

Be filled, it urges. *Take heart*, it commands. The world is more than you know, more than you see. There is, at work every hour, a layer of beauty and truth and infinite wisdom. Its name is grace.

Motherprayer: The Holy Work of Paying Attention

As I sift through the grains of my week, of my year, of my long stretch of motherhood, I've come to know that the grains I hold a bit longer, the grains I hold up to the light, are the fine, simple hours that come, often, right after school, or tucked into tight spots at the oddest of times.

When the boys I love are bothered, are troubled, are weighed down with the grit of the day.

When suddenly the chairs at the table are pulled. Bottoms splot onto cane-woven seats. When teacups are cradled in palms. When oranges are peeled, piled in sections.

When the talking begins.

Of all the scores of things I might do in a week, in a lifetime, nothing perhaps matches the wholeness of those holy hours.

The boys I love are sifting through their own hearts, laying their troubles at my chest, at my heart. They are trusting not my mouth but my ears.

Just listen, you can hear them hoping.

When days are bad, when hours are bumpy, most of the time we aren't looking for quick cures or Band-Aids. All we want, really, is someone to sop up the hurt. To listen to worries.

All we want, often, are eyes that look deep, look gently. Eyes that listen. Not words that cut off. Not words that dismiss.

Just hear me, you can hear the hearts saying. If you listen. Just listen.

The quieter I sit, the more wholly I take in the words, the deeper the place from which the words come. It's a curious algebra, the one of the heart.

In fact, the art of listening is a most active one. You take in, you sift, you turn each morsel of thought, you examine, allow the questions to rise. But you wait. You hold your questions off to the side, in a queue, on hold. Patiently waiting their turn.

When it's time, when the pause comes, you reel out the questions, one, or maybe a string. You sit and you wait.

A question, constructed with care, unspooled on the river of talk, is one that sinks deep, one that says, *I am with you in thought. We are in this together. Our heads and our hearts entwined, teamed up. You're not alone. I wonder too.*

No solution need come. No answers, plucked from the current.

In that holy interlude when one heart's ache is offered up, received by another, the weight shared, burden lifted, those are the hours that matter the most. Those are the hours that answer our prayers. The ones we've prayed all our lives.

The child, apparently, has no clue that his entire life long we have been listening, listening intently. We have felt the piercing upon impact of certain words as they simultaneously hit our eardrums and zing straight to our hearts. They have no clue that we have powers of instant memorization, that we tumble some lines, the occasional shard of a word or words, over and over and over in our minds that don't cease, don't know from the pause button.

And, without his even saying a word sometimes, the someone who loves him, who knows him so deeply, she is able to tiptoe into his bedroom at night, on just the right night, and she knows to slip under the sheets, right beside him, and start making those circles on his forehead, the ones that he loves, the ones that make him let down his shoulders, his worries, after a long hard day. And she knows, without his saying a word, just when he needs her to ask, "So how was your day, sweetie?" because she might have asked that question a dozen times already, but it's at bedtime, it's there in the dark, when the words serve to uncork the deep heart of the matter.

Mamas know those things.

They do if they are listening, if they are paying attention. If their own hearts are still enough, if they've spent years deep at work practicing the art of those things that mamas do and know and say and understand and feel through and through.

In the end, mothering is all about the particulars. Mothering, at its best, is the art of paying pure attention.

And Sometimes We Must Wait for the Harvest of What We've Sown

I realized that what we do, in the long, long years of planting, is we are merely sowers of the seed. We scatter all life long, the bits of truth, of hope, the few scant things we know.

We scatter as we turn the words, in conversation after conversation. We poke a fertile nugget deep into the soil as we take our children by the hand, show them places and faces unlike the ones they would otherwise know.

We sprinkle seed through the books we read them when we pull them on our lap, turn pages. And then, years later, leave bound offerings tucked beneath their pillow, just in case they find a minute for inhaling thought before they fall to sleep.

And after all the sowing, I realized, we can only stand back. Pray for rain and sunlight. Keep watch on what's out where we have laid our lifetime's crops.

Hmm, is that a little bit of green, poking through the loamy soil? Is that a tendril, reaching for the sky?

We'll not know the harvest for some time. But we will trust that all the planting, tending, praying was not in vain.

Some seasons, what comes up is rich, is plenty, fills the bins. Some seasons, what you put into the ground isn't what comes up at all.

But there will be a reaping. And, God willing, it will be more than you had ever counted on.

That's the way it is when it comes to growing a thinking child. We've no flame to simply light their way, only seeds to scatter on their path, and wait—and hope—for blossoming to come.

A Centenary of Blessing, of Deep and Undying Thank-You

Enchanted by Celtic and Jewish and Ignatian understanding that we are called to anoint the holy hours of our every day with blessing—one hundred blessings precisely, as instructed in Jewish teaching—I decided to unspool my own centenary of thanks across the arc of a day.

In this season of bountiful thanks, as we gather roots from the ground, and fowl from the field, I march through time, sewing blessing into the whole cloth of my day. (It's a long way to 100, so you might want to take this in doses, a swallow here, another there.)

In the liminal landscape between asleep and awake, thank you, Holy One, for heart still beating, for breath, for first thought, the one that tickles us into consciousness. Thank you for darkness before the dawn, morning after morning a reawakening to the metaphor, the truth, that in our darkest hour we might hold on just one more minute, for surely the stars will dim, and horizon's edge will be doused in tourmaline and tangerine, and finally radiant gold.

Thank you, by the way, for celestial paint set.

Thank you for bed, and blanket. Thank you for the one I love who lies beside me, whose breathing I know by heart. Thank you for the lump that's warm, that's there when I reach across sheets in the night, in the morning. Thank you for deepening love and the long winding road that brought him to me, to my heart.

Thank you for the dawn itself, that sacred cloak of in-between, when crescent moon dangles just above, but night gives way to morning's light, and heaven's dome, at the seam of earth and sky, soaks up scant threads of all-absorbent amber rose. Thank you for the stillest hour when all that moves is barest breeze that rustles leaves, and far off, the stirrings of the lake that never cease.

Thank you for this old house, with arthritic floorboards, ones that creak at just the same juncture, with just the same footfall. Thank you for kitchen, and heat that is cranked. Thank you for whiny old cat there at the door. Thank you for coffee beans and hissing pot, and the old chipped mug that fits snug in my palms.

Dear Maker of All That's Blessed, thank you for the sound of those footsteps clomping onto the floorboards above, and the certitude that—so far this day—all is well. Thank you for shower, hot and pulsing and shaking off sleepy-eyed resistance to standing upright.

Thank you for porridge I stir at the cookstove. Thank you for the sustenance I dollop in spoonfuls, the alchemy of cooking for those we fuel for the day. Thank you for faith in the vespers unfurled, in between handfuls of raisins and walnuts and jewel-toned dried fruits, the ones we toss with abandon into the bubbling pot.

Thank you for clementines, and sugary cinnamon. Thank you for butter, slathered and melted. Thank you for school bus drivers who wait. Thank you for the click of the door when at last the morning rush is over, is ended, and no one is reaching for car keys, muttering under her breath.

Thank you, Blanketer of Wonder, for the quiet stitched into the morning's hours, the quiet so thick I can drink in the tick and the tock of a grandfather's clock. And the squawk of the blue jay, and the chatter of sparrows.

Thank you for work to be done. Thank you for dishes piled in the sink, whose scrubbing and rinsing gives me a moment to think, to ponder the day. Thank you for typewriter keys that call me and fingers that play on the alphabet rows. Thank you for sentences that write themselves, and words that are birthed from deep down inside.

Thank you for wisdom, the sort that comes in unexpected flashes, when you only know you've found it as you feel your heart go thumpety-thump, and you sit bolt upright, or feel the goose bumps sprout up and down unsuspecting flesh. That wisdom might come reading along the pages of news, or in a poem slipped under your transom, or from a stranger passing by. Plenty often, it comes through the holy gospel of a wonder child, as you catch one last phrase tossed over a shoulder at the schoolhouse door.

Thank you for all that's poetry—wisdom-steeped or just plain beautiful, breathtaking. And thank you for gospel of any order—be it birthed from holy child, everyday saint, or even the so-called kook who stands on the street corner, proclaiming through a megaphone.

Thank you, yes, for telephones, for that rare sound of a voice that nestles against the tenderest heart. That, within the first breath of the very first syllable, brings comfort, collapses miles and aloneness, amplifies the hours absorbed in coming to this holy bond of deep knowing each other, inside and through.

Thank you even for the bits of news—of whatever ilk, good or bad or nasty—that percolate the hours of each day, make one slice of time so vastly different from the next, stitch drama to the script of life, offer us the chance to absorb each and every frame from an angle never before perceived.

Thank you, most of all, for the deep down knowing that you, Holy Depth and Gentleness, never leave me adrift. Never let my quakings take me down. Ever bring me light, and tender touches. Ever hold me up, against the chilling winds. And bring me to communion with all that's glorious and bountiful in this rugged, rugged landscape.

I might be among the few who salute the cloudy skies of November on my long list of thanks. Ah, but those angora gray skies, they comfort me, harbor me. I'll take the somnolence, the introspection of a gray day any day. So thank you for cloudy and gray.

And I'd be remiss if I didn't mention how thankful I am for hearts that continue to tick, day in and day out, despite the trials we toss their way, as we worry and fret, then, without notice, shriek in deep joy and excitement. Poor ol' heart, the one that landed in me anyway, it might not have realized it was signed on for a roller-coaster ride of such seismic proportion.

Speaking of ticking, thank you for the schoolhouse clock that does just that, minute by minute, hour upon hour, heartbeat against the wall.

Thank you, too, for windows. And for the flutterings and flashes just beyond the glass, as clouds of gentle creatures take off and land, from sky to limb and back again—each time, lifting just a little bit of my soul.

Thank you for doors, the ones that let in unexpected someones, someones we love. And keep out the wind and the cold.

Thank you for fires that roar and logs that crackle. Thank you for the one that's turning the so-called keeping room, across from the kitchen, into a chamber of flickering gold. Thank you for the two lumps under blankets, snoozing by the fire as I sit here, now typing.

Thank you, Lighter of Night, for the cloak of darkness that comes early now, velvety backdrop for twinkling of stars, and moon that holds me, most every eve, in its trance.

Thank you for dusk, dear Lighter of Light, the far edge of the day, beginning of nightfall, when the last seeds of illumination are scattered, are rosy.

Thank you for dinner hour, and the blessing of slow-simmering stew. Thank you for the bounty of greens from your earth, and spices from pods and seeds and stamens.

Thank you, God, for the trees and the gnarly limbs, and the hummingbird now buried deep in my garden.

Thank you for candlelight. And the lights of your making: moonlight and sunlight and dappled radiance scattered like seed across the landscape. Thank you for twinkling stars and streaking ones too—chalk marks etched across the slate of the night sky.

Thank you for drifting off to sleep, and dreams that color our imagination. Thank you even for revelations that come to us in the awful interludes of tossing and turning. Thank you for wanting to wake up again, to climb from the bed. Thank you for the blankets we tuck under the chin of our sleeping child.

Thank you, dear God, for the child. For the breathtaking chance to infuse all that's good in this world. Thank you for lessons taught while holding a hand, or wiping a tear. Thank you for Band-Aids that quell the hurt, and words that do the same. Thank you for everyone who lifts up our child, the teachers who inspire, the coaches who are kind. And the lady down the block who never fails to plant a fat, wet kiss on that child's pink cheek.

Thank you for the year drawing to a close, and this pause to nod our heads and whisper gratitude. Thank you for the kaleidoscope of turning season, the ever-shifting call to attention. Thank you for crunching leaves, and tumbling snowflake.

Thank you for love in all its iterations. For birth, and death, and all that animates the interstitial hours. Thank you for those who walk beside us, who put a hand to the small of our back, or reach out to carry us across the bottomless abyss. (And that's 100.)

Thank you, God, for all of this. And more. So, so much more.

The Autumnal Kitchen

Soon as that molasses sunlight dribbles in across the kitchen windowsill, I'm hauling out the pots and pans. I'm chopping. Stirring. Inhaling deeply. I'm strangling circulation at my wrists and forearms, dangling bags far too heavy, too many, as I troll the farmer's market, come harvest time. Harvest time: When pumpkins delight, and zucchini threaten to maim with their record-breaking heft. Pears, piled high, recline, blushing all the while. And apples by the bushel beg for a root cellar back at the old homestead. Maybe, just maybe, one last stubborn tomato ripens on the vine. And, wise to this waning succulence, this savoring, you waste not a drop. You fill the larder. You relish, indeed you do.

Aunt Brooke's Cranberry-Pear Relish

Apt, this dish named relish. Must be because you can't help but lick the spoon. You relish it, the relish. Its majesty came to me by way of my Upper East Side sister-in-law, the so-titled Aunt Brooke, who, with four hungry boys, knows her way around the kitchen. She turns out capital-D Delicious, and her stock-in-trade defense, often: "It's a cinch." This time, she was straight-talking. Slice, dump, wait. That's about the whole of it. But what emerges is a pot of garnet-jeweled deliciousness. And at our house, it's now synonymous with all that's best about the autumn kitchen. We serve it straight through to Christmastime, long as there's a pear waiting to be sliced and whole cranberries willing to succumb to the cookstove's sultry steam bath.

Provenance: This gem, a family heirloom from Aunt Brooke, a baker extraordinaire, who dabbles splendidly in cooking, and who is known to the world as Brooke Kamin Rapaport. She long ago acquired this from her Great-Aunt Eleanor Serinksy.

Yield: Enough to fill a medium-sized serving bowl (I often double the recipe, since more is always wanted.)

    3 Bosc pears, unripened, unpeeled
    1 (12-ounce) package whole cranberries
    ½ cup water
    ½ cup to ¾ cup granulated sugar

The art here is in the pear slicing, so keep the slices slender, allowing the curves to tempt.

Toss into pot with lid.

Rinse and dump bag of cranberries atop pears in pot.

Add water and sugar. Stir but once, taking care not to ravage the pretty pears.

Cover, cook on medium flame or heat.

Listen closely. When you hear the pop-pop-pop from beneath the domed lid (about 7 to 10 minutes), turn off heat, and let the magic do its thing.

Peek in after 15 to 20 minutes. Behold the garnet-hued heap. Stir gently.

Serve at room temperature, or tuck into the fridge and allow anywhere from half hour to overnight for thickening to occur.

You'll relish it, all right. Might be a side dish on a groaning board or atop pound cake with a dollop of vanilla-bean ice cream. You'll lick your lips—the very definition of "to relish."

Cure-All Mac and Cheese

When the bee stings, or the homesick blues need quelling, this oozy spoonful of deliciousness belongs in a mama's tin of kitchen cure-alls. It's the ubiquitous remedy at our house for any ailment in the book. (And one or two make-believe ones, besides.)

Provenance: *Gourmet* magazine, May 1995

Yield: Serves 8 children

> 3 tablespoons unsalted butter
> 3½ tablespoons all-purpose flour
> ½ teaspoon paprika
> 3 cups milk
> I teaspoon salt
> ¾ pound pasta, tubes or wagon wheels or whatever shape suits your fancy (a tube—penne or rigatoni, among the many—fills with the cheesy sauce and makes a fine, pillowy bite)
> 10 ounces sharp cheddar cheese, shredded coarsely (about 2¾ cups)
> I cup coarse, fresh bread crumbs, coarse
> ¼ cup (or more) Parmesan cheese shavings

Preheat oven to 375 degrees Fahrenheit, and butter a 2-quart shallow baking dish (the broader the crust, the better).

In a 6-quart pot, bring 5 quarts salted water to a boil for cooking pasta.

In a heavy saucepan, melt butter over moderately low heat, and stir in flour and paprika. Cook roux, whisking, 3 minutes; then whisk in milk and salt. Bring sauce to a boil, whisking, and simmer, whisking occasionally, 3 minutes. Remove pan from heat.

Stir pasta into pot of boiling water and boil, stirring occasionally, until *al dente*. Drain pasta in a colander, and in a large bowl stir together pasta, sauce, and 2 cups cheddar cheese. Transfer mixture to prepared dish. *Macaroni and cheese may be prepared up to this point 1 day ahead and chilled, covered tightly (an indispensable trick when confronting a serious to-do list for a day of, say, birthday or holiday jollity).*

In a small bowl, toss remaining ¾ cup cheddar with bread crumbs and sprinkle over pasta mixture, topping it all with a downpour of Parmesan shavings (a heavy hand with the cheese is never a bad thing, certainly not at my house where my boys insist I do so, preferring their cheese to supersede bread crumbs).

Bake macaroni and cheese in middle of oven for 25 to 30 minutes, or until golden and bubbling. Let stand 10 minutes before serving. At last: dig in.

Wintertime

Season of Stillness

*T*he wisdom of winter is that it beckons us to seek the light, truest light. Enwrapped in darkness, the kindled flame burns deep within. Ember at the heart of stillness, it's elusive, plays catch-me-if-you-can. We need to quiet the cacophony, attune our souls to the silence of snow falling, of celestial pin dots blinking in the long shadow of night. Only then might we bask in the white-winter glow, the radiant light of Christmastide. Only then might we carve out a birthing place for what's most holy. In depth of winter, we're called to heighten our senses of wonder, of expectant vigil. Keep watch, is but one instruction. Be still, yet another. It's in the deep stillness that we might hear the sacred whisper, the one that infuses our motherheart, turns our hours of expectation, of waiting, of longing, into blessed offering, one that burns from the true heart of love. As we count toward the most silent of nights, we're wise to behold the immeasurable gifts woven into the everyday, most especially the babes we've cradled from the beginning. And will love till beyond the end.

Wintertime's Wonderlist

it's the season of . . .

kindling candlewicks, flame-by-flame, ancient armament against the inky darkness . . .

traipsing to the woods, hauling home the sacrificial fir to be adorned in paper chains and tinsel, and a lifetime's accumulation of hand-me-down treasures . . .

flour-dusted countertops on the afternoon my grandma's famed cut-out cookies demand to be rolled and baked and iced, then tucked for (short-lived) safekeeping in wax-paper blanketed tins (see recipe, page 75) . . .

scarlet-feathered incandescence aflame against the white-on-white tableau . . .

curling into the couch, under the red buffalo-check blanket, with O. Henry's "The Gift of the Magi," the Christmas classic that forever defines the art of selfless giving . . .

brown-paper packages tied up with red-plaid ribbons . . .

tiptoeing into the dawn to deliver, by Radio Flyer sled, holiday loaves and love notes to all the neighbors' back stoops . . .

making room on the mantle for baby Jesus . . .

scribble your own wintertime wonders here . . .

A Count-Your-Blessings Calendar

Blessed Be Wintertime, Season of Stillness

WINTER SOLSTICE: As the solstice brings on winter, celebrate the darkness. Make a bonfire or simply light candles. Throw a log in the fireplace, listen to the crackle. Tradition has it that fires are sparked on the longest night to help the sun get its job done. Give thought to the life that's birthed out of darkness.

BLESSING 2: Savor the winter's dawn especially, in all its stillness. Not a leaf fluttering, not a blue jay's squawk or sparrow's chirp. Listen for the still, small voice that's best attended to when quiet at last envelops us.

BLESSING 3: We have watched, for weeks now, the slow undressing of the world beyond the sill. There is no hiding in the depth of winter. We battle back darkness with the kindling of the lights, and the stringing of branches with all the glitter we can gather. Look within for truest light.

BLESSING 4: Spying the brown-paper packages, tied up in red-plaid ribbons, all stacked under the fir tree, put thought to Elizabeth Barrett Browning's certainty: "God's gifts put man's best dreams to shame."

CHRISTMAS DAY (DEC. 25): On the morn of Nativity, wrap yourself in newborn wonder. Awake before anyone else. Light a candle. Look out the window and quietly count your blessings.

BOXING DAY (DEC. 26): Quiet and dark are invited in, not whisked away, come the season of stillness. Be hushed. Punctuate your afternoon's walk with a trail of birdseed sprinkled from winter-coat pockets. Take supper by the fire—or near a cove of candles. Fuel on simple soup and sturdy bread. Read stories by firelight. Tuck children in their beds, while grown-ups keep vigil deep into the night.

BLESSING 7: Be blanketed in the holy lull that is the first snowfall.

BLESSING 8: Revel in the child's joys of deep-freeze winter: Candy canes and marshmallows populating steamy mugs of hot cocoa, the only hope for luring frost-nipped limbs in from out-of-doors. Consider it sweetened invitation to deepened conversation.

BLESSING 9: "I love the dark hours of my being / for they deepen my senses . . . / From them I've come to know that I have room / for a second life, timeless and wide."—Rainer Maria Rilke, Bohemian-Austrian poet (1875–1926).1

BLESSING 10: Morning incantations at the cookstove: Stir a pot of oatmeal—bejeweled with dried fruits from the pantry—for the people we love, still tucked under the covers. Blanket each dreamer in blessings for the day, as you draw the spoon through bubbling porridge.

BLESSING 11: Survival seed, you might call it. Imbued with animation and sparks of magic, surely. Not a minute

*after it's been dumped, the yard's aswirl with sound and
stirrings. On days of arctic chill, it's the least we can do,
to stoke the hearts and bellies of the
birds who give flight to the day, who
fill the boughs and branches with their
scarlet feathers.*

*BLESSING 12: Pick up a well-thumbed copy of Mary
Oliver's* Red Bird, *and drink in her rare brand of poetry.*[2]

*BLESSING 13: Delight in the winged thespians of winter:
Keep watch on the flurry of winter's birds coming in for
a landing at the feeder, taking turns, shooshing each other
away. Ponder this: "Birds are a miracle because they prove to
us there is a finer, simpler state of being which we may strive to attain."
—Douglas Coupland, Canadian novelist.*

*NEW YEAR'S EVE (DEC. 31): "Don't ask what the world needs. Ask
yourself what makes you come alive and go out and do that, because what the world
needs is people who have come alive."—Howard Thurman, author, theologian, civil
rights leader (1899–1981).*

December's Sacred Invitation

*T*here is something about December, all right.

And I call it a gift.

It might be my ancient Celtic roots, or maybe it's my monastic inclinations, but give me a gray day, a day shrouded in mist and peekaboo light. Give me a shadowed nook to slip into. And I wrap myself in the cloak of utter contentment.

It's dark all right, come December, month of the longest night, when minute by minute our dot on the globe is darkening.

Yet darkness to me is alluring; it calls me to turn inside, to be hushed, to pay attention.

Mine is a lonely outpost.

December, most everyone else complains, is unbroken darkness. And they're grinding their teeth when they say it.

The way I see it, though, maybe the *saddest* thing is, we've blinded ourselves to the darkness. Cut ourselves off from the God-given ebb and the flow of darkness and light. It's poetry, the rise and the fall of incandescence and shadow, measured in lumens per square foot. But, mostly, it's lost on us—bright lights, big city.

When's the last time you tiptoed out your kitchen door—or onto a fire escape—and took in the sky show? It's there every night: the stars and the moon, waxing or waning, a night-after-night lesson in fractions. Lesson in wonder.

I say, celebrate the darkness—landscape of discovery, of finding our way only by engaging, igniting, heightening our deeper senses, the senses of the heart and the soul, the intellect and the imagination.

The truth is: darkness draws out our deep-down depths. Darkness is womb, is seed underground. Darkness is where birthing begins, incubator of unseen stirring, essential and fundamental growing.

December, I like to think, is when God cloaks the world— or at least the northern half of the globe—in what amounts to a prayer shawl. December's darkness invites us inward, the deepening spiral—paradoxical spiral—we deepen to ascend, we vault from new depths.

At nightfall in December, at that blessed in-between hour, when the last seeds of illumination are scattered, and the stars turn on— all at once as if the caretakers of wonder have flown through the heavens sparking the wicks—we too, huddled in our kitchens or circled round our dining room tables, we strike the match. We kindle the flame. We shatter darkness with all the light we can muster.

The liturgical calendar, prescriptive in its wisdoms, lights the way: it gives us Advent, season of anticipation, of awaiting, of holding our breath for spectacular coming. Season of dappling the darkness with candled crescendo.

And therein is the sacred instruction for the month: make the light be from you. Deep within you.

Seize the month. Reclaim the days. Employ ardent counter-culturism, and do not succumb.

Abraham Joshua Heschel, the great Jewish thinker and one of my heroes, talks about Shabbat—every week's holy Sabbath pause—as erecting the cathedral of time, the Jewish equivalent of sacred architecture, only for Jews it's the sanctification of time, not space. Writes Heschel: "Learn how to consecrate sanctuaries that emerge from the magnificent stream of a year."[3] I say, build yourself a tucked-away chapel, a humble half hour's chamber of silence, of prayer, of deepening.

Here's a radical thought, for December or otherwise: live sacramentally—yes, always. But most emphatically in the month of December.

What do I mean? To be sacramental is to lift even the most ordinary moments into Holiness. Weave the liturgical into the everyday. Look to Jesus, for starters. Bread and wine, everyday agrarian foodstuffs, he made into the most sacred sacramental feast.

Live sacramentally: sit down to a dinner table—even dinner for one—set with intention. Ditch fast food. Embrace all that's slow. And with purpose. Light candles at dinner. Light the Advent wreath. And if you're Jewish, blaze the menorah. If you're Jewish and Catholic, as my family is, well bring on the fire battalion, we're lighting every which flame.

A dear friend of mine laughs about being a person of "smells and bells," and by that he means a certain affinity for the burning of incense and chiming of carillons. The candle, the tintinnabulation of the bells, it sets off a deep-down stirring in a Catholic or an Anglican of certain age, it echoes of our not-*so*-distant past. And what I love about the coining of that phrase, "the smells and the bells," when I pause and really think about it, is that it reminds me that deep in the heart of our spiritual DNA, we are hard-wired to respond to the liturgical, to pulse with reverence at a life lived sacramentally, slowly, marveling at the magnificence, yes, at each and every turn.

Maybe we're most purely and purposefully alive when we turn our backs to—press against—a guzzled-down life that pays no attention, that goes with the flow, that "kills a few hours," that takes all of it, any of it, for granted.

And why? Why are we screeching the brakes, dialing down all the noise?

Because this is our one chance at December this year—and who knows how many Decembers we might have?

December is invitation. December is God whispering, "Please.

Come. Closer. Discover abundance within. Marvel at the gifts I've bestowed." Listen for the pulsing questions within, the ones that beg—finally—to be asked, to be answered. Am I doing what I love? Am I living the life I was so meant to live? Am I savoring, or simply slogging along?

December is invitation. Glance out the window. Behold the silence of the first snowfall. Stand under heaven's dome, and watch the star-stitched wonder: Orion, Polaris. Listen for the love songs of the Great Horned Owl. Be dazzled. Pray the prayer of bedazzlement.

Mary Oliver, the poet saint, tells us, "attentiveness is the root of all prayer." And reminds us that our one task as we walk the snow-crusted woods or startle to the night cry of the sky-crossing goose is "learning to be astonished."

Ever astonished.

Renaissance scholar and poet Kimberly Johnson says, "I want to live my life in epiphany."

So do I.

Maybe, so do you.

And December, at the cusp of winter, season of fury and stillness, December demands our attention. It is a month draped in myth and legend. It is a month that rings with the power of the simplest story, the one we wait for—childlike, rapt, noses pressed to the window, scanning the heavens for bright and shining light.

December invites us be our most radiant selves. And we

find that radiance deep down in the heart of the darkness. The darkness, our chambered nautilus of prayer. The coiled depths in which we turn in silence, to await the still small voice that whispers the original love song. Chorus and refrain, inscribed by the One who Breathed the First Breath.

Advent Meditations

Practicing Advent

I am practicing Advent. Really practicing. Paying attention. Giving in to the season in ways that wash over me, seep into me, bring me back home to a place I may never have been.

Like a child this year, I have a just-opened sense of these days.

I am, for the very first time, not counting down. Not ticking off days and errands to run, like a clock wound, really, too tightly.

Instead, I am counting in a whole other way. I am counting, yes, but the thing that I'm doing is making count each one of the days.

I am counting the days in a way that takes time. That takes it and holds it. Savors it. Sucks out the marrow of each blessed hour.

I am, this year, embracing the darkness. I am kindling lights. I am practicing quiet. I am shutting out noise, and filling my house with the sounds of the season that call me.

I am practicing no. *No* is the word that I'm saying to much of the madness. No, I cannot go there. No, I cannot race from one end of town to the other. No, I will not.

I am practicing yes.

Yes, I will wake up early. Will tiptoe alone, and in quiet, to down in the kitchen, and on out to the place where the moon shines. Where the early bird isn't yet risen. But I am. I am alone with the dark and the calm, and I am standing there watching the shadows, the lace of the moon. I am listening for words that fill up my heart. It's a prayer and it comes to me, fills my lungs, as I breathe in cold air, the air of December, December's most blessed breath.

The darkness itself offers the gift. Each day, the darkness comes sooner, comes deeper, comes blacker than ink. It draws us in, into our homes, yes, but more so, into our souls.

It invites us: light a light. Wrap a blanket. Sit by the fire. Stare into the flames and onto the last dying embers.

Consider the coming of Christmas.

I am preparing a room at the inn. The inn, of course, is my heart.

Stillness

Curious thing this December, more than ever, it is the stillness that speaks to me. That I seek.

I am practicing the art of being still.

Stillness, when you look for it, is never far away, and not too hard to grasp.

I find, though, it takes a dose of concentration. And sometimes a stern reminder; I mumble to myself, "Be still now."

It is Advent, the counting-down time, the something-coming time of darkest winter. And, in my good spells, I am deeply, urgently, savoring the getting there.

It is, as it so often is, my littlest one who softens me, who stirs me back to stillness, who insists we not forget to give the twisty fir its drink. Who takes me by the hand. Who asks his big, wise brother if he too "checked Advent" (meaning did he yet dig out his daily dose of duly-numbered sweet, from the red-plaid pockets strung across the window panes, I through 24).

It is, nearly as deeply, the thick meringue of snow bending all the branches. It is the flash of scarlet feather at the window. It is the sound of orange peel simmering. And the tinkling of the spoon scraping at the bottom of the cocoa-filled mug.

These are the things that make for stillness, or rather, the keys on the ring that might unlock it after all.

It is, in fact, the heart, the soul, that are the vessels of pure true stillness: those chambers deep inside us that allow for the holy to unfold. The birthing rooms, perhaps, of our most essential stirrings.

To be at one with all that matters. To begin the pulse-beat there where the quiet settles in and the knowing reigns.

It is, yes, in the stillness that the sacred comes.

A Mother's Advent: Awaiting

In the abyss that plunges between two cliffs—uncertainty (will he be safe?) and certainty (of course he is safe)—I engaged in the ancient and timeless art of waiting.

To wait, sometimes, is to be pregnant with hope. Sometimes, to wait is to dread. But that's not the case, not really, when it's a child you birthed, fourteen short years ago, who is out in the world, and it's dark and it's late and you would like once again to hear the clomp of his feet sloshing snow on the rug in the hall.

To this particular species of waiting, you realize quickly, you are quite new, quite unaccustomed. You only just now are getting a taste of the trials that come with the letting out of the spool that, until now, until high school, you kept rather close to the palm of your hand.

The art of waiting for someone you love, someone to please come home, is an art that has lost some of its power here in the day of the cellular tether. Worried? Give a call. Can't find? Cell can.

Back through the history of time, though, there has been waiting and waiting. Penelope waited for Odysseus. Civil War mothers waited for soldier sons. And now I, a mother whose son had just lost his cell phone, waited for mine.

Odd thing, the book that was waiting with me, the book I was allegedly reading, the book whose words my eyes glanced at but didn't take in, not so much anyway, was a book with a passage on waiting.

As the clock ticked ever so slowly, I passed again over the letters spilled there on the page.

This time I read:

> Waiting, because it will always be with us, can be made a work of art, and the season of Advent invites us to underscore and understand with a new patience that very feminine state of being, waiting.
>
> Our masculine world wants to blast away waiting from our lives. . . . We equate waiting with wasting. So we build Concorde airplanes, drink instant coffee, roll out green plastic and call it turf, and reach for the phone before we reach for the pen. The more life asks us to wait, the more we anxiously hurry.[4]

The author of these words is Gertrud Mueller Nelson, whose 1986 book, *To Dance with God*, is a treatise on ritual and one of those rare books that offers more, plentiful more, with each reading.

She encourages us to practice the art of waiting, the art of delayed gratification. Our children, most of all, need to practice and practice, she urges. And this time before Christmas, this time when the world is rushing so madly, she suggests in a deeply countercultural challenge, is the peak time to settle in and make the most of the incubation that begs our attention.

"Brewing, baking, simmering, fermenting, ripening, germinating, gestating are the feminine processes of becoming and they are the symbolic states of being which belong in a life of value, necessary to transformation," Nelson writes.

And I listen.

Is not the slowing of time, and the quickening of attention, the whole point of our practice here? Are we not, day after day, looking to slow the E-Z, the instant, the world without pause?

Are we not the stewards of every hour allotted to that holy thing we call Our One and Only Life, and are we not wisest when we behold its every sublimity—its light, its shadow, its gradations in between—slowly and certainly and savoringly?

Prayer with Pots and Pans: Antidote to December Doldrums

I did the surest thing I know to beat back the mid-December blues: I cranked the oven. I hauled an armload of oranges from the fridge. Grabbed the canisters of flour and sugar. Soon found myself slamming my grandma's rolling pin against a sack of walnuts (therapy with a mighty bang). Already, I was starting to feel a little oomph in my kitchen dance. I grated. I measured and dumped. I inhaled the sweet scent of orange. Delighted at the garnet bits of berry swimming through the mixing bowl of batter. I was baking my way to Christmas. And on the way, I found my merry heart.

There is something deeply therapeutic about not just baking, but baking *en masse*. Making like you're a factory of one. I lined up all my baking pans. Buttered, floured, in one long sweep. I found it much less onerous to tick through required steps in quadruplicate, so much more satisfying than one measly loaf at a time. There was some degree of superpower in seeing my butcher-block counter lined in shiny tins, a whole parade of Christmas possibility. I found a magic in the multiples. In not just joy times one, but joy by the dozen.

Psst. Here's the recipe (from Gourmet *magazine, via epicurious.com) that got me started. I vamped, as always, from there: more orange zest, more nuts.*

Cranberry Nut Bread

Yield: Makes 1 loaf (though I'd heartily recommend doubling or tripling till you've baked for every house on your block)

2 cups all-purpose flour

1 cup sugar

1 ½ teaspoons double-acting baking powder

1 teaspoon salt

½ teaspoon baking soda

1 stick (½ cup) cold unsalted butter, cut into bits

1 teaspoon freshly grated orange zest

¾ cup fresh orange juice

1 large egg

1 cup coarsely chopped cranberries

⅓ cup coarsely chopped walnuts

In a food processor or using a bowl and a pastry blender, blend together flour, sugar, baking powder, salt, baking soda, and butter until the mixture resembles meal; then transfer the mixture to a large bowl.

In a small bowl whisk together zest, juice, and egg; add to the flour mixture, and stir the batter until just combined.

Stir in cranberries and walnuts, and transfer the batter to a well-buttered 9-by-5-inch loaf pan.

Bake in the middle of a preheated 350-degree-Fahrenheit oven for 1¼ hours, or until a toothpick comes out clean.

Let bread cool in the pan for 15 minutes, and turn it out onto a rack.

Inhale the pure joy of having baked your way to holiday bliss. Wrap each loaf in shiny tin foil, tie with a floppy, red grosgrain bow (or silver or gold or Hanukkah blue). Tiptoe into the cold, and commence your delivery. You'll be humming before you get home. And that's a fine December's promise.

The Holy Pause Is upon Us

*I*t is the holiest pause of the year for me, the birth of new light, just after the longest, darkest night. The quiet that comes, I imagine, just as it came in the manger long, long ago. I imagine the mother with child. I imagine her belly, hard, ready to birth. I imagine the cows lowing, and the sheep, the soft sounds of a barn, mixed with the muffled wail of pain from a mother in labor. Then stillness. Holy stillness. Silent night. And then, at last, that cry from the deep, from the newborn lungs of the babe, the sound of God shattering the night. The first sound, a cry.

It's a story that draws me deep into the folds of its threads. It's a story that startles me, tenders me, year after year. It's a story I need in double doses this year. And so I will tell myself the story over and over. I will stand at the edge of my crèche and marvel at the newborn tenderness. I will marvel at the courage and strength of the mother who birthed her firstborn, her one and only, in the dim chill of a barn, surrounded by the murmurations of those beasts of burden. I will imagine the night sky, jet black, stitched with shimmering knots of pure light.

I will take hold of that tenderness, that courage and strength, and make it mine. Or try, anyway. I will scoop up the seed that is Christmas, and tuck it deep in my heart. I will breathe into it, allow it to grow, to blossom, to spill beyond these few short days when the pause, holy pause, is upon us.

The holy pause is the most blessed gift of Christmas.

A Prayer for Christmas Coming

A s is my way of keeping Christmas, I will bow my head at the dawn, and I will whisper my litany of prayerfulness. It's the essence of Christmas to me: to weave the strands of petition into a whole and mighty salutation to the God who looks to us to uphold tenderness, mercy, and most of all justice. The God who begs us to keep peace here on this most blessed globe, the one of mountains and majesty, fragile bog and feathered flock. The God who gave us this gift with the undying hope that we'd hold it close to our hearts, and never let it shatter.

Here is my prayer, or at least the first draft of it:

(The more insistent the prayer, the earlier I seem to rise. And so this morning, the heavens are star-strewn still, the edge of the dome is soaked still in inky black. The cardinals haven't yet stirred from wherever it is they sleep.

And yet, my heart is bubbling. My prayers rise up from deep inside. They can't wait to take flight, to be put to the airborne parabola, the one that puts wings to their breath.)

I pray for the mothers who have buried a child, the mothers for whom Christmas will never be whole, will ever be hollow. I pray and pray for peace, just a thread of it, to come to them, to wrap for a moment around their aching heart. I pray for one moment's relief from the stinging emptiness that will not be staunched.

I pray for the children who've lost their mother, two in particular I know and love, and countless others I've read about, countless others who cling to the margins of all the merriment, knowing it's a country to which they no longer belong. For children without a mother on Christmas, there is no peace, no everlasting peace.

I pray for war-torn cities and towns and faraway places shorn of all hope. I pray for the children hovering in the cold. I pray for the bodies of the babies disentombed from the rubble, the dust of hatred dropped from the skies. I pray for the mothers and fathers, I pray for the men and the women—cold, hopeless, hungry. I pray for the masses left to die, awaiting the words—any words—that tell them the world is listening, has heard their cries, awaiting the word that the world is coming, hope is coming to save them.

I pray for world leaders courageous enough to have opened their borders, to let in the rivers of refugees, disgorged from their homes, from their histories, from any shred of a sense that they're safe.

I pray for the weary souls I see lying under puffy-layered sleeping bags, or threadbare blankets, or thrown-away boxes, on cold hard sidewalks, under viaducts, against the grates at the base of shimmering downtown towers.

I pray for my children. I pray that in their hours of darkness, the light comes. That they see how brilliantly they shimmer in the landscape of my heart and my soul. I pray that someday they understand just how wholly they have filled me, how they put purpose to my being alive. That each and every day we try and try again to teach each other: this is how you love.

I pray for all of us who, more often than not of late, feel hollowed. Feel jarred and broken by the hatred spewing all around. I pray for our tender hearts and fragile spirits. I pray that we don't topple. And if we do, I pray for someone strong to come along, to reach out a hand, to whisper hope, and pull us to our feet.

I pray for those who haven't a clue how deeply they teach me each and every day—be it a story on the news, or one passing by in the social media whirl. Or someone I bump into at the grocery store, or riding on the el, or shivering in the cold as I shuffle down the sidewalk.

I pray for the ones we've lost this year, the ones whose words rumble through my head, through my heart, each and every day. I pray especially for my friend who wrote these words: "Wake up every morning acknowledging just how much beauty is in your world. Pay attention to it, honor it, and keep your heart and your eyes wide open. You won't regret it," she promised.

I pray for the poets and wordsmiths and makers of art in every form—in clay, in thread, in wood, in every hue under the sun and the moon. I pray for those words that catch against my heart, and work their way into prayer. Those words that leap from my soul into the heavens.

I pray for the God who catches them, who catches the words of the prayer, who catches us all.

More mightily than any prayer I pray of late, I beg Holy God not to abandon us now. Not to leave us to our sins and our shattered promises. I promise to love a little bit harder, to live a little bit better, more true to the blessing I was made to be.

And this is the prayer I pray most mightily: I promise to love, God, and I beg you to show us—show me, show every single lost and hungry one of us—the way. The holy, certain way . . .

Thank you.

Amen.

Silent Night Awakening

A rms wide open, it's the dawn that follows the silent night. Night of awe. Dawn of darkness lifting. The dawn, I pray, when the outlines of all your blessings come sharply, crisply, indelibly into focus.

When, perhaps, you find yourself all alone, nestled inside the flutterings of your heart and your soul, and all the Christmases of all the years before come tumbling softly, and this particular one, perhaps, leaps out from the pile because this is the Christmas when you've unwrapped a particular glimmering knowing from under your tree.

Maybe it's the simmering of newfound love. Maybe it's the weight finally shrugged off your shoulders. Maybe, after all the hours of darkness, you've found your way to the flickering light off in the distance, and you're home now, finally home.

Maybe it's that the story of Christmas—the Blessed Virgin

Mother and Holy Child, the newborn babe laid in the straw, the star of wonder lighting the heavens, the beasts of the pasture poking their noses into the barn, drawn by all of the stirrings—maybe the story of Christmas this year awakens a place deep inside you that's too long been numb to the hope, and the light, that Nativity brings. That Nativity lays quietly at the cusp of your heart.

Come, open the gift. Open the possibility of wonder. Of glistening light. Wrap yourself, for even just this one sacred hour, in the hush and the whisper of peace. Peace on earth, please. But peace in your very own kingdom—you can make that happen if you take hold of wonder, if you chase out the noise, if you close your eyes (or open them wider than ever) and open your heart. Breathe deep. Inhale the Divine, animator of all that's wonder-filled, that's breathtaking.

That's what I pray you find this blessed morning, under your tree, tucked in your heart. May this dawn of quiet at last, this day-breaking hour of stillness, seep deep into your every channel of wonder, into the depth and breadth and whole of your soul and fill you with Christmas at its holiest.

Amen. And merry blessed Christmas.

Motherprayer on a Cold Winter's Morn

Not for one minute could I send my kid out into the cold, back to school, back to streets where a gang war wages, and not do the feeble things a mama does: I slathered mustard on bread, I folded slices of deli turkey, I tucked it all in the little brown bag he uses day after day. I prayed the whole while. I prayed mightily.

When he tumbled down the stairs and saw me standing there with my mustard knife in hand, he looked surprised. "Mommo, what are you doing here?"

Just packing lunch, was all I said. He knows me well, my kid of twenty-two years. He knew without me saying so that that sandwich was superpacked. Stacked with prayer upon prayer. Besides the turkey.

As I closed the door behind him, as I told him I loved him, called out, "Be safe," I traced a sign of the cross onto the back of his thick winter coat. It's all I could do.

It's the truth of motherhood, or one of them anyway: we're

armed with so very little. Especially when up against a world of flying, piercing, life-taking bullets.

Yet we don't abandon our station: we rise before the dawn, we shuffle down the stairs, we do what little we can. We pack a lunch, with a mother lode of prayer.

We are pulled by heart out of slumber. We are pulled by heart into prayer. Deep into prayer.

Radiant Brokenness: The Cracks Where Light Comes In

Someone I love was shattered this week. It shattered me.

And it got me to thinking about *kintsugi*, the Japanese art of repair when a bowl or a vessel is shattered. In this craft as ancient—and poetic—as any still practiced on earth, the crack isn't simply glued, the pieces reassembled. It isn't hoped that no one will notice, that the brokenness will be hidden, kept secret.

Hardly.

The crack and its repair are illuminated. Literally. Powdered gold, most often, but sometimes silver or platinum, is sprinkled into lacquer resin. The vessel is veined boldly, radiantly. If a piece of the vessel has been shattered into splinters, the missing piece—the absence or abyss—becomes invitation for abundant gold compound, a gilt vein pooling into eddy or island or pond. Golden pond of patching together.

Kintsugi. Golden joinery.

It's the art of embracing brokenness. It's craft, yes, but even more so it's philosophy, a philosophy that draws from the Japanese understanding of *wabi-sabi*, which is to behold the beautiful in imperfection, impermanence.

At heart, it's a knowing that the fracture doesn't mark the end of the object's life, but rather embodies an essential moment in its history. It's worn because it's been woven into the fabric of daily life, and daily life offers up bumps and bruises and tears and tatters. The more it's engaged in the depths of day after day, the more likely it'll be knocked around, jostled, sometimes even broken.

So, too, the human heart.

To be engaged in the drama of the human theatre—that place called being alive—is to be exposed to shattering.

Yet isn't the redemption found in the truth—resounding truth—of Ernest Hemingway's glorious line from *A Farewell to Arms*:

> The world breaks everyone and afterward many are strong in the broken places.

Or, in the infinite wisdom of Rumi, the Sufi mystic:

> The wound is the place where the Light enters you.

So that, today, is my prayer. That the shards disassembled, strewn and scattered across the plains of life, in those darkest hours known to humankind, are not merely slapped back into some smoothed-over order, some half-baked pass at hiding away the fracture.

But that, as inspired by Buddhist wisdom, we come to a deep understanding of the truth of golden joinery. That if perhaps we can find love for the whole of who we are—the broken, the fractured, the piece that's forever lost—we might discover not simply strength but radiance in the stuff we find to patch ourselves back into a whole.

And in so doing we become all the more beautiful because of where we've been broken. And where the Light now finds a way in.

The Aches of Letting Go and Leave-Taking: Mother Whisper, Mother Tears

Of late, the pangs come often, come hard. I miss him already. I long for these days, and they're not even gone yet.

It's a trick of the brain, a trick of the heart. And it's not just a trick for the mamas among us. All of us, every one, we know what it is to miss someone we love before they're not here anymore.

It's the thing, is it not, that churns deep in our souls, propels us to love and love deeper. To cherish. To know, in our blood, with the swirls of our fingertips even, that what's in our midst is sacred, is holy, is never forever.

I'll savor each drop of each day. And know, soon enough, I'll be ever so thirsty. And my sweet little boy will be big. Too big for my hip. But never my heart. Which grows right along with him.

I always think, I've never my fill of him. Never enough of his stories. Never enough of his heart.

Never, ever enough.

We wait, some sweet homecoming moments, for the light to come in through the distance. And then, on the other end of the dizzying spell of squeezing a hand that's grown far bigger than ours, and bending low for a kiss to the brow of the sleeping man who's back in his old twin bed, on the other end of shoulder pressed against shoulder at the cookstove, or plopping on the edge of each other's bed for one or two thoughts shared in the dark, there comes the hour when the light pulls away, into the darkness again.

And so, in the space in between, we immerse ourselves deep in the holiest way to live: at full and piercing attention. Stripping away the parts of ourselves that might otherwise get in our way . . .

So it goes, when there's only so much time—and you're graced with the knowledge that, soon as it begins, it's tumbling toward the close. You shrug off all the little things that don't matter. You set your divining rod to high alert. And you whirl through the short spell—the too-short spell—of too-few hours and change (including sleep time), and you inhale as if through a double-wide straw.

Which, from time to time, is a very fine way to practice the art of being alive. As if the edges of your consciousness were bordered with a high-voltage fence. Where, if you drifted into unconsciousness, into not paying attention, a wee zap to the noggin would jostle you back into full-throttle live-in-the-moment.

The Blessings of Deep-Breathing Motherlove

I wished for one thing my whole life long: that through trial and error, and stumble and fall, and mistake after blunder, I might over time figure out how to live and breathe love in a way that was purely contagious, that spread like a rash.

If we find it within ourselves to love even one human being in this limitless, boundless, inexhaustible yet exhausting way, can we not take that same instrument, that very same heart, and apply those very same lessons beyond the hearts of the ones we call our own—our children, by virtue of birth, love, or circumstance?

Mothering, it's the stuff of literature, yes, and holy text, indeed. And it stands as sure a chance as there might ever be for one sacred calling to change the course of history.

Imagine the child who is deeply and unconditionally loved. Imagine who that child might grow up to be. And consider the cumulative power of a life spent absorbing love's truest, deepest lessons. Lessons of courage. Of forgiveness. Of compassion. Of tirelessly looking out for the ones at the margins, the ones who need a guardian angel.

Mothering with full and open heart stands a very fine chance of propelling wholeness, goodness, mercy into this blessed world. It carries the possibility that we might be the best that we can be, but also that those we love might be.

The truest truth of parenthood, or at least the truest one for me, is that every stitch along this broadcloth of hope and faith and unwavering trust is one knotted with prayer.

Prayer for a Still Winter's Morning

*H*ow did the heavens know? How did the Great Beyond know that I needed a morning's blanket?

I needed stillness to step into.

The night had been long, had been tumbled. It was one of those nights when worry stitches each one of your dreams. You awake, yes, but you wonder if you've slept even a wink.

All you need on a morning like that is softness. Is quiet. You need a world on its tiptoes, padded tiptoes. You need a morning that, like an old friend, understands without words. Sidles up beside you, lays its head on your shoulder. Breathes.

The morning comes softly. Snow tumbles down in flakes that shift from fat to fatter. You breathe. You inhale blessing, breath after breath, and then you let loose, your morning's litany, petition spiraling atop petition.

Dear God, watch over him. Dear God, protect her. Dear God, forgive us; forgive us our endless offenses, our trespasses, too. Dear God, forgive this globe that seems to be spinning too close to the edge of madness.

Dear God, fill us with grace. Give us strength. Give us wisdom. And, please, for once, let words fall from our lips with half the sense we'd hoped they would hold.

Dear God, blanket us. Open our eyes and our hearts. Show us the way. Let us startle someone in these hours ahead with some blast of unheralded goodness. Let us be the instrument of your peace. Let us pass over temptation, not be the one to whisper the word that would cut to the quick. Not turn the cold shoulder.

Dear God, steady us. Deepen us. Let me be the vessel this day that carries you into the midst of the chaos. Let me sow love. Let me bring pardon. Let me, in these hours ahead, scatter faith wherever there's doubt; hope, in place of despair.

You've answered my prayer before I've opened my eyes for the day. You've laced the dawn in white upon white, you've hushed the world out my window. You've opened my door into prayer—still heart, deep vow, bold promise.

Dear God, I thank you. Now let us tiptoe softly into this day.

A Mother's Benediction

A nd so our children someday soar. That's the hope, therein lies the heart of motherprayer. As our young take flight, we cast our eyes toward heaven's dome, tracing a trajectory—*their* trajectory—beyond our reach, perhaps, but never, ever, beyond our hearts.

Blessed be the winds that gyre and eddy beneath their wings, and the holy breath that enwraps us, carries us, infuses us, on this epic flight that is mothering. May our motherheart ever pulse with prayer. And may our polestar be love beyond measure, far beyond the journey's end.

Amen.

The Wintertime Kitchen

*P*lunged into the longest night, when darkness blankets the hours and celestial timekeeper tells us winter's solstice is upon us, the kitchen isn't merely a place for distraction; it's downright prescriptive. Crank the flame, steam up the panes of the windows, the ones where each morning Jack Frost leaves icy inscription. While bears retreat to their caves, we humans clang pots and baking pans. We stir. We sift. We make swirls out of buttery frosting. And we fill tins upon tins. Overstock the fridge while we're at it. 'Tis the season for indulgence of the highest order: extra places squeezed along the table, every chair in the house pulled up to the groaning board. Company's coming. Best of all, the ones you love most.

Welcome-Home Brisket

When you're about to welcome home your far-flung child, or anyone you love—be it the kindled holidays of darkest December or any old homecoming any time of the year—and you want the whole kitchen bewitched by the heavenly vapors that rise from a long, slow oven. And if you're a believer, besides, in the lung-filling olfactory embrace that begins the instant the door's cracked ajar, before you even wrap your arms round the shoulders you've so longed to squeeze with all your might . . .

Provenance: My friend Harlene Ellin's mom, whose prescription I follow religiously

Yield: Depends on how hungry you are, but you'd be safe to guess this will feed 6.

> 3 pounds first-cut brisket (Such things a Catholic girl must learn; who knew from first-, second-, or even third-cut?)
> 1 cup Heinz Chili Sauce*
> ½ cup brown sugar
> ¼ cup dry red wine*
> ¼ cup water
> 1 small or medium onion, sliced
> 3 cloves, whole
> 6 black peppercorns, whole
> 3 bay leaves

* If you're making this Kosher for Passover, you'll need to swap Kosher-for-Passover ketchup for the chili sauce

(for zing, add ¼ teaspoon garlic powder, ¼ teaspoon onion powder, and ½ teaspoon chili powder), and be sure to use Kosher-for-Passover wine. (A Hanukkah brisket demands no such Passover proscriptions.)

Rinse brisket and pat dry with paper towels. Preheat oven to 325 degrees Fahrenheit. In a small bowl combine chili sauce, brown sugar, wine, and water. Mix well. Pour ¼ of chili sauce mixture into a roasting pan. Place brisket on sauce, fat side up. Place onions, cloves, peppercorns, and bay leaves evenly over brisket. Top with remaining chili sauce mixture.

Cover roasting pan tightly with foil. Bake brisket for 50 to 55 minutes per pound, or until meat is fork tender. (Pay attention to the math, friends; it makes for a long, slow roasting. A 3-pound brisket will roast for at least 2 ½ hours.)

Remove meat from pan, and place it in a container. Remove bay leaves, peppercorns, and cloves from gravy, and put gravy in another container. Refrigerate meat and gravy, separately, for several hours or overnight.

To reheat brisket, slice against the grain to desired thickness, and place in a covered casserole dish coated with cooking-oil spray. Remove and discard any congealed fat from gravy. Pour the gravy over the meat. Cover and reheat in a 375-degree-Fahrenheit oven for 30 minutes or until heated through. (Brisket can be reheated in a microwave.) In a word: mmmm.

A Christmas Gift . . .

Christmas Eve Elves' French Toast

It's been tradition, long as I can remember, that, come Christmas morn, I'm first one out from under the bedsheets. I've been known to take two steps at a leap, to plug in the tree, and get to work in the kitchen. For years, that meant Christmas-y coffeecake, à la page 337 of the highly splattered Silver Palate Good Times Cookbook. *But then I enlisted the Christmas Eve elves. In short, their magic trick is this: overnight soak, swift slide in the oven, and—poof!—rising cloud of cinnamon, yolk, and butter. Suddenly, I discovered more time for sitting alone under the tree. And, with far less fuss, the vapors seeping from the oven smelled just as get-out-of-bed as that yeasty rise, on a morning when eager boys need little stirring to spring from under the covers. It's pure prestidigitation, too, on any snowy morn, when those who snooze in your beds need an extra dollop of oomph to arise and seize the day.*

Provenance: Inspired by a long-ago recipe in the *Chicago Tribune*, though my own fiddling at the cookstove might make this unrecognizable from the original.

Yield: One 9-by-13 casserole

> 1 loaf challah (the braided egg bread, or whatever holiday loaf strikes your fancy), cut into eight 1-inch-thick slices, or however many snugly fit your 9-by-13 baking dish
> 2 cups whole milk
> 1 cup cream (it's Christmas, after all)
> 8 large eggs

> 4 teaspoons sugar
> 1 tablespoon best vanilla extract
> Few shakes cinnamon
> 1 orange, grated (if you're so inspired)
> ¾ teaspoon salt
> ½ cup dried fruits (the jeweled bits of garnet cranberries, plump apricots, make the bake dressed-up enough for Christmas)
> 2 tablespoons butter, cut into small pieces
> Powdered sugar, for dusting
> Maple syrup, honey, or your best Christmas-y jam

Generously butter 9-by-13-inch baking dish.

Layer bread slices across bottom of dish so it's completely covered and filled to the top.

In a separate bowl, mix milk, cream, eggs, sugar, vanilla, cinnamon, orange rind, and salt.

Pour over bread. Toss in a handful of dried fruits, tucking in between and under bread slices.

Cover with foil.

Refrigerate, covered, overnight. (This is where the Christmas Eve elves come in.)

Next morning, preheat oven to 350 degrees Fahrenheit.

Remove egg-cream-bread heavenliness from refrigerator and uncover; it's not necessary to bring casserole to room temperature. Dot the top with butter.

Bake uncovered until puffed and golden, 45 to 50 minutes.

Let stand 5 minutes before serving.

Dust with powdered sugar,
and serve with maple syrup, honey, jam,
or whatever sweet stokes your sugarplum
dreams. Merry, merry, but of course . . .

Afterword

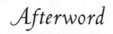

A Short List of Sacred Instruction

Upon spiraling across the year, we end as we began, with two instructions:

Love as you would be loved.
Live as if there's no promise of tomorrow.

And this:

Pay deep attention.
Behold the beauty and the blessedness.
Breathe love into your motherheart. Let every crack and crevice fill with radiant light. Then turn and pour it on the world: the ones you call your own, yes, but more so—and emphatically—those who dwell beyond.

Notes

A Few Books You Might Want to Pull from a Shelf

Newborn Year

1. Robert Ellsberg, ed., *Dorothy Day: Selected Writings* (Maryknoll, NY: Orbis, 2005), xxxvi.

Springtime

1. Barbara Cooney, *Miss Rumphius* (New York: Viking Penguin, 1982).

Summertime

1. Ann Voskamp, *The Broken Way: A Daring Path into the Abundant Life* (Grand Rapids, MI: Zondervan, 2016), 72.
2. Mary Oliver, "Drifting," in *Blue Horses: Poems* (New York: Penguin, 2014), 53.
3. Mary Oliver, "Little Summer Poem Touching the Subject of Faith," in *West Wind: Poems and Prose Poems* (Boston: Houghton Mifflin, 1997), 36.

Autumn

1. Rabbi Sylvan Kamens and Rabbi Jack Riemer, "A Litany of Remembrance" in *Gates of Repentance: The New Union Prayerbook for*

the Days of Awe (New York: Central Conference of American Rabbis, 1996), 490–91.

2. Abraham Joshua Heschel, "On Prayer," in *Moral Grandeur and Spiritual Audacity: Essays*, ed. Susannah Heschel (New York: Farrar, Straus and Giroux, 1996), 258.

3. Blessed be the souls of those two dear friends who died too soon, and whose words live on forever: Cecilia Vaisman (1961–2015) and Mary Ellen Sullivan (1959–2016).

Wintertime

1. Rainer Maria Rilke, *Prayers of a Young Poet*, trans. Mark S. Burrows (Brewster, MA: Paraclete, 2013), 24.

2. Mary Oliver, *Red Bird: Poems* (Boston: Beacon, 2008).

3. Abraham Joshua Heschel, *The Sabbath* (New York: Farrar, Straus and Giroux, 1951), 8.

4. Gertrud Mueller Nelson, *To Dance with God: Family Ritual and Community Celebration* (Mahwah, NJ: Paulist, 1986), 62.

More from Barbara Mahany

Capture the Beauty of Small Moments, and Unravel the Mysteries of Mothering

Motherprayer: Lessons in Loving
Hardcover ISBN: 9781501827273

In Barb's six-week, in-depth Bible study on Mahany celebrates the essence of what mothers do: a way of loving that becomes prayer beyond words. Personal love letters on the gifts of mothering, interspersed with family recipes and gentle essays, offer beautiful lessons in how to love, and how to love well. In her bracingly honest style, Mahany captures the ephemeral moments of motherhood—the hard, the glorious, the laughter, and the tears—and invites readers to pay attention, cradle our loved ones in prayer, and see the sacred lessons in loving.

Make Room for God and Illuminate the Godly Specks

Slowing Time: Seeing the Sacred Outside Your Kitchen Door
Paperback ISBN: 9781426776427

Mahany, invites readers to discern the divine in the ordinary moments of everyday and live an examined life where everything is a form of prayer. By probing deeply the nooks and crannies of the home-front, the author points out that the reader need not venture far to find what matters most.

Read Sample Chapters, Listen to Author Reading Excerpts, and Find Shareable Images and Info at AbingdonPress.com/BarbaraMahany

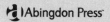
Abingdon Press